JAMES DURAND

AN ABLE SEAMAN OF 1812

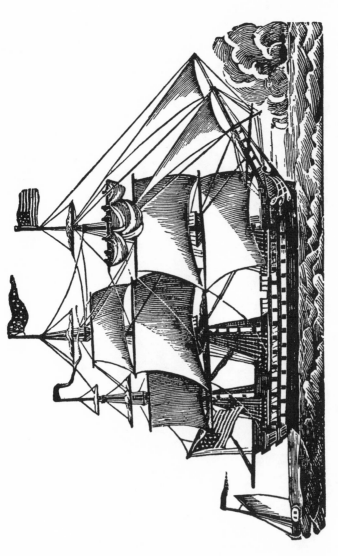

THE UNITED STATES FRIGATE *CONSTITUTION*

This picture was printed on the back of the 1820 edition of Durand's narrative. It was engraved on wood and stereotypes were sold to printers by some New York type-founder. The present illustration is from a photograph of a type-founder's specimen, furnished by courtesy of the Typographic Library and Museum, Jersey City.

THE LIFE
and ADVENTURES
OF JAMES R.
DURAND

DURING A PERIOD OF FIFTEEN YEARS,
FROM 1801 TO 1816 : IN WHICH TIME HE WAS
IMPRESSED ON BOARD THE BRITISH FLEET,
AND HELD IN DETESTABLE BONDAGE FOR
MORE THAN SEVEN YEARS.

WRITTEN BY HIMSELF

BOOKS

CHAPMAN
BILLIES
INCORPORATED
SANDWICH MA

This book was first published in 1820 in Rochester, N.Y., by James Durand, the author. The edition at hand is based on one edited, and containing ancillary essays, by George S. Brooks which was published by Yale University Press in 1926 as *JAMES DURAND*.

Manufactured in the United States of America

This edition published in 1995 by
Chapman Billies, Inc.
Box 819, Sandwich, MA 02563.

ISBN 0-939218-08-9

COMMODORE JOHN RODGERS
Redrawn by T. Diedricksen from the *Polyanthos*, Boston,
October, 1813.

Foreword.

=====

JAMES DURAND'S *journal tells us the story
of one of the many thousands of American
boys who turned to the sea for a livelihood in the
latter part of the Eighteenth Century. At eleven
years of age the unhappy little fellow first knew
sea-sickness, home-sickness, abuse, and lack of
proper food. As boy and man he was small of stature but dauntless of spirit. He experienced shipwreck and privation, saw the massacre of the whites
in Haiti, often felt the cat-o'-nine-tails, and was
once a member of a mutinous crew. He tried to win
his way to the quarter deck, served on three American war vessels—including the U.S.S.* Constitution*—was taken prisoner of war, and then impressed into the British Naval Service. For seven
years he served under that then hated flag. His
worst suffering of all was in the War of 1812 on
board H.B.M.'s frigate* Narcissus. *They were ordered to attack Stonington, Connecticut, where he
had relations. He informed the Captain that he
would not fight against his native land. Two other
Americans stood by him. The Captain "ordered
the boatswain to make three halters. 'I will hang
these damned rascals,' he said. The halters were*

accordingly made and put about our necks. Then he gave us fifteen minutes to change our minds and agree to fight. We would not change our minds. So then he ordered the master to put us in irons and keep us on maggoty bread and water until we complied with his commands. So we were put in irons."

Those were bullying, brutal, bloody years in naval life under any flag. Durand's crudely written journal gives us a close-up picture of them. Supplemented by Mr. Brooks' illuminating footnotes, it makes an intensely interesting story. The bitter feeling of those days has passed away with the men of that generation, happily for the two great English-speaking nations. All intangible that remains are the glorious traditions of courage on the sanded decks and in the fighting-tops of our naval vessels, of the thrilling escapades of the little privateers and the small boats manned by our Yankee seamen. All that still floats of the gallant squadrons of one hundred and more years ago is the old Constitution, *with her halo of victory. She is the memorial of the courage and sacrifice of Durand and all other American sailormen of his time. It should be a privilege for every man, woman, and child who enjoys the freedom of our Flag to help to preserve her for the inspiration of future generations.*

HERBERT L. SATTERLEE.

July 19, 1926.

Contents.

NEW LONDON FROM MANWARING'S HILL

From an engraving probably *ca.* 1812 in the possession of
P. LeRoy Harwood, Esq., New London.

Introduction.

IT is very evident that this story was written some years after the events chronicled. Durand was frequently mistaken about his dates, which is not remarkable as he had only his memory to identify an incident with a particular day or year.

If the work has a value, it is in the picture of the times and conditions of which its author treated. Source material seems to show that Durand's story is a fairly accurate engraving of a part of American society, a century and a quarter ago. The particulars which are substantiated by contemporary writers are discussed on the pages following the narrative.

After all, the difference between 1801 and 1926 is mainly mechanical. It is a putting of gossip upon telegraph wires, a reliance upon the word of the "Daily Times" instead of upon the thoughts of the Presbyterian minister, a fear of taxi bandits replacing the terror of wild Indians, and a system of transportation that makes a trip from New York to Washington an after-dinner incident instead of a prolonged adventure.

Every bitter comment upon the enemy which Durand made was repeated in more lurid terms by members of the recent American Expeditionary Forces. Every provincialism he muttered may be matched by to-day's speakers at the lunch clubs. Every violence shown to unfortunate prisoners can be duplicated in the day's news during the past ten years; in the American Army prison in Paris, the Southern convict camps, the actions of special policemen during strikes.

In short, Durand's narrative shows that, so far as the humanities are concerned, mankind is like the Bourbons in exile—"learning and forgetting nothing."

Durand added a touch of unintentional humor to his narrative, by his lack of appreciation of the importance of some of the scenes he witnessed. He saw Napoleon at Gorée, at the time when the Emperor of the French was making Europe tremble. With Yankee eyes, Durand noticed that "he wore an indifferent hat. . . ."

His attitude was like that of the American Signal Sergeant who, in October of 1918, squatted on a hilltop and watched the effect of the greatest artillery barrage ever laid. History was being made at the cost of incalculable thousands of dollars a minute. The Signal Sergeant saw the barrage smother the concrete, earth, and wire defenses of the Hindenberg line. He saw regiments of artillery with their guns parked hub to hub, firing almost as rapidly as machine guns. He saw waiting infantry counted by thousands instead of as individuals.

The Signal Sergeant was looking at the greatest man-made spectacle the world has ever seen; one that rivaled nature in destructive force and vastness. And the Signal Sergeant watched it with the same Yankee shrewdness that gleamed in Durand's eyes as he appraised Napoleon's uniform.

"If you could get the hot dog concession for this army, and get enough dogs and rolls, what a hell of a lot of money you could make," sighed the Signal Sergeant.

We may believe that the German poet Goethe was the only witness of the Battle of Valmy who appreciated its deep significance. Neither the Prussian officers nor the emigrant noblemen who swept down through the passes of the Argonne, nor the officers of the Revolutionary levies who met and defeated them at Valmy, September 20, 1792, on that day realized the importance of the battle. Yet on those few thousand men depended all the political concerns of modern Europe; for the winning of that battle made it possible for the French Revolution to live.

Only Goethe, riding across the field as his knees shook with "cannon fever," sensed this. That night, at the Prussian mess, he said, "From this place and this day forth commences a new era in the world's history. You can all say you were present at its birth."

No such prophetic vision was granted James R. Durand, Able Seaman. He saw the United States, through her puny navy, shatter the power of the Mediterranean pirates and win from Great Britain a grudging recognition as an equal world power.

Yet Durand wrote of the food given the sailors by

the pirate bey; of the seamen who were flogged
through the fleet; of the cost of the rockets that were
fired at Stonington.

G. S. B.

New York, 1926.

JAMES R. DURAND

AN ABLE SEAMAN OF 1812

Voyages to the West-Indies and the Slaves' Rebellion at Port-au-Prince

I WAS born December 1, 1786 in the town of
Milford, County of New Haven, State of Connecticut, where I lived until I was six years old. My
parents having a large family, my elder brother
and I were bound apprentices to a farmer* for a
term of five years. We stayed there in the town of
Washington for the term of our apprenticeship
without any occurrence worthy of remark.

We then returned to Milford resolved to go to
sea.

On our return, we found our relations all in good
health and tarried with them a few days. Then we
went to New Haven, a town eight miles distant
from Milford. There we took a packet and arrived
at New York. After tarrying seven days without
an offer to our satisfaction, we put back to New
Haven. My brother here shipped for sea. I, however, found employ in a packet for nearly three
months.

* See note 1, page 87.

But here my misfortunes intervened. A severe soreness prevailing in my left foot, I thought I would return to my friends in Milford, as I had no relations in New Haven. My mind being unsteady and young, without direction, I resolved to quit the seas, go to Milford and live with my uncle. He was a man of business, keeping a grocery, yet withall a man of steady character as will appear when I tell that he had been a selectman for seven years or more. With him I actually found a home and a friend.* He wished me to tarry with him, offering me every indulgence I ought to wish for. But my mind was still unsettled in spite of my being fifteen years of age, so I again resolved to try the seas.† I left my uncle's house in the year 1801 and repaired to New Haven.

It was in the month of September. I being in good health and spirits, was enticed away by Capt. Smith who was going on an intended short voyage to Charlestown, South Carolina.

In agreeing with the captain about my wages, he informed me that he already had a boy at a rate of six dollars a month, but that if I could go aloft (viz: from deck to mast head) in less time than the boy could, he would pay me eight dollars. Accordingly, having done so, I agreed for that sum.‡

* See note 2, page 88.
† See note 3, page 88.
‡ See note 4, page 90.

The Storm.

WE sailed in November, 1801 for Charlestown. We stopped in New York for two or three days and then proceeded on our voyage. On a Thursday, we reached a place called the Horse-Shoe. There we lay all night. On the following day, we weighed anchor and proceeded on our voyage.

It is often remarked among sailors that to sail on Friday is ominous of ill-luck, which proved to be the case with us. Although in the morning the wind was fair and blew a pleasant breeze from the N.E., it shifted about 2 P.M. and blew a very heavy gale for three days.

On the third day, the seas ran mountains high and one of them struck our larboard quarter, broke the quarter rail in three places and washed overboard twelve barrels of apples. These apples belonged to the company as a venture and were of more value to us than our wages. This accident happened in the forepart of the day. In the afternoon came our second alarm. The mate went to sound the pump.

"All hands to the pump," he sung out. "There's three feet of water in the hold."

This was enough to make any seaman tremble and as for me, who was unaccustomed to the seas, it made me resolve I would never again set foot on a deck, if I reached land in safety. But this wishing and resolving was all in vain. I went to the pump and continued there until the hold was clear of water, which was about eight hours. I was very wet, but so much in want of sleep from excessive fatigue, that I lay down to sleep without removing my wet clothes.

The wind continued to blow violently for four days more. It forced us out into the Gulf stream, where the sea was so contrary and our ship so leaky that we were in danger of being lost. Then there arose a thunder storm which was the most violent I ever witnessed. It appeared as if the whole world were ablaze.

Towards night, we observed several dim lights in the shrouds and on the yards.

"What is the cause?" I asked the Captain.

"It is an omen of good weather," he replied.

So it turned out. By the sixth day the weather was pretty moderate. We arrived at Charlestown after a voyage of ten days. Here we disposed of our cargo, consisting of butter, cheese, potatoes, apples, onions and cider. Then we hauled our vessel up, high and dry, for repairs and found her very rotten. We repaired her and took freight to Georgetown. Then our ship sailed for the West Indies in the month of January 1802.

We had on board 34 head of cattle, 30 sheep and

18 hogs. By the Captain's advice, I now took a venture in the cargo, the interest being deducted from my wages. We had a cargo of lumber.

So we put to sea: we found no heavy wind but a great calm, so that we made but one mile in eight days. Our cargo of lumber, being put in the hold wet, heated there. It made our drinking water so bad that the water would string like soft soap in the dippers or buckets. As a consequence, we all suffered greatly. However, we got a breeze at last and arrived safe at Martinico, in the harbor of Port Royal, after a passage of thirty-seven days.

A Speculation in Oranges.

As soon as we arrived, the Captain went ashore to try the market and the crew went for water. I, being the youngest, was left on board to keep ship. A boat came alongside, with much fruit for sale. Having no money, I was tempted to barter some of the ship's provisions for oranges and bananas, of which I ate so many that I was sick and came down with a fever that lasted eighteen days. It was a just reward for taking the ship's provisions and was a final cure for my ever attempting the like again.

We found no sale for our cargo there, so we set sail for Dominico. Here we hove to the brig and the Captain went on shore. During his absence there came an English man of war boat along side to over-haul the ship's crew.* All had protections but myself and my sickness was my protection (as they would not impress a sick person for their service). Our Captain returned and we sailed to Merchant Bay on the same island. There we sold our cattle.

The cattle were very poor, owing to the great length of our passage. One of them had actually died of starvation. This one the Captain had ordered us to barrel; which same he sold to the negroes for ten $, although I was confident the beef would not have weighed 30 pounds, exclusive of the bones.

Here also we disposed of the rest of our cargo, took in some ballast then went to St. Kitts where we took on more ballast and a great number of oranges. I purchased five hundred myself for eighteen pence a hundred. After a passage of ten days we reached Georgetown. I sold my fruit at the advanced price of five $ per hundred.

We fitted up our vessel, painted her and got ready for sea. Before we got any cargo on board, the Captain thought proper to smoke her for the destruction of rats. We were gratified to find we had killed some hundreds. I mention this as being entirely new to me.

* See note 5, page 90.

With cattle on board, we sailed for the West-Indies. Eight days out to sea, we were overtaken by a dreadful thunder storm which commenced in the after part of the day and continued until two o'clock in the morning. In the course of the night we were greatly alarmed by the cry of "Fire."

Our cabin was stored full of casks and dried pease. The Captain being fearful of their taking damage from water, put a tarpauling over as well as the companion leaf, in order to secure them from the rain. However our cook was drunk and a lighted candle which he set in the transom, fell off setting fire to a spare sail.

When it was discovered, the fire had become so furious as to burst the cabin door and the flames ascended half-mast high. Notwithstanding this, the Captain made a full spring into the cabin, got hold of the sail which was not yet wholly consumed, and with our assistance, brought it on deck. Then we threw it overboard and suppressed the remainder of the fire by throwing on water.

Although the Captain's arms were severely burned up to his shoulders, he was not the only sufferer. He ordered the cook to be lashed up to the main rigging and gave him one of the soundest floggings I ever witnessed.

Before the night was over, we were alarmed by a new and serious adventure. A flash of lightning split our jib boom in two and thence passed into our fore-castle where it killed some sheep and hogs.

I was aloft at the time and I found myself totally deprived of sight for the space of twenty minutes. On recovering, I came down on deck. A very heavy sea attended the thunder and lightning. We were all anxious for the day which soon appeared.

At Martinico, in the town of St. Pierre, we sold our stock. We made other voyages from Charlestown to the West-Indies but had no misadventures worth recounting, until one time when we sailed to a place called Port-au-Prince.

A Sailor's View of the Negro Rebellion.

WE stayed there five weeks and there I beheld the most horrid sight which my eyes were ever to witness.*

This island was inhabited by the French who had there a great many black slaves; at least five blacks to every white man. The slaves were not satisfied with their condition, so at the instigation of the English, resolved upon a general massacre of the whites. One day while I was on shore I hired a black man for a quarter-of-a-dollar to show me to the spot where a hundred and twenty whites had been put to death at one time.

* See note 6, page 92.

8

All these bodies had been put into one hole and lay uncovered. I observed bodies of infants of both sexes there as well as the remains of persons of various ages, exposed in every shape that cruelty could suggest.

At this time, an American ship, bound for New York, had taken on her cargo and was ready to sail. On the day of sailing, the Captain took some men, women and children on board so that he could carry them away and help them to escape a certain death. The Captain went on shore to get the ship's clearance.

About nine o'clock in the morning, the ship loosed her fore-top-sail and fired a gun as a signal for sea. Upon which the commander of the fort came along side and demanded permission to search the ship. In the Captain's absence, the mate ordered them to keep off and fired upon them when they did not obey. At this they returned with a large armed force, boarded the ship and found the refugees concealed on board.

These poor people they tied hand and foot, together with the mate, took them on shore and hung them all on the hay scales without form or trial. The Captain wished to revenge the death of his mate, but had not sufficient force, so he sailed away.

As we were bartering our cargo for coffee, we were obliged to remain there a month longer.

9

One morning, there came alongside a lieutenant of one of the privateers which belonged to the fort. He asked for the use of our long boat, which was loaned to him with the understanding that it should be returned quickly. So we put out the boat and they towed it ashore. Some time in the night they filled the boat with men, women and children, took them outside the harbor mouth and drowned them all. The boat was returned to us next day.

Another time, our Captain ordered four of us to take him ashore in the jolly boat. We observed a great collection of people about the guard house. We joined the crowd in order to satisfy our curiosity. We saw there a mulatto man standing with his hands tied behind him. We learned he was a prisoner, about to be shot. Accordingly we thought proper to tarry a little and witness the execution.

They marched him a little way over a brook. The privateers men were drawn up to shoot him. Seven soldiers were stationed in front and seven on each side.

The prisoner requested the liberty to give the command to fire himself, which the officers granted. He next asked permission to drink a glass of rum before he died. His hands were then untied and a glass of rum given him. He drank the health of all the bystanders, broke his glass and commanded the soldiers to shoulder arms.

They did this with some inaccuracy. He then ordered them to do it over again. They did it more carefully and he commanded them, "Fire." He fell pierced with five musket balls.

His crime was upsetting a boat and drowning three women and two children. I thought it extraordinary to see the unconcern with which he gave the word for his own execution.

Shortly after this, we got ready our loading, in company with eleven other sail. We came to the Porto Plat and as there were some ships lying there belonging to the United States we came to anchor until they were ready for sea the following day. We now put to sea again, homeward bound.

We had not been long out of port before we fell in with two French privateers, bearing down upon our convoy, which had sixteen sail.

Our captains managed their ships so well we gave one privateer a broadside that dismasted her.* Shortly after we discovered another French privateer and then spoke to an English privateer and informed her of the French sail which was then lying to leeward. She chased her several times through our fleet. I counted sixty-five guns discharged at her; however I knew nothing of the effect they had on her.

* See note 7, page 94.

11

We were favored with a short passage, only five days from land to land. I brought with me five hundred weight of coffee which I sold for twenty-five $ per hundred which added to my monthly wages for seven months gave me four-hundred-and-five $.

I now tarried six weeks on shore to study navigation. But I had not made all requisite proficiency before I shipped on the *Nonpareil,* bound to the same place, Port-au-Prince. After eight days passage, we saw a brig on the leeward, which appeared to be in distress. Our Captain ordered us to sail there to carry relief. But to our astonishment, we found her to be a French privateer. The help we gave them was a broadside. Then we hauled our wind and in two hours we were out of sight.

When we got our cargo ready in Port-au-Prince the Captain called me aside and asked me if I dared go ashore to help him steal away an old man, his wife and daughter. I told my Captain that I thought this a proper purpose, to get white people out of the reach of these horrid murderous blacks.

Accordingly, I went on shore, prepared as he had directed me.

Three Escape the Massacre.

I CARRIED a spare sailor's clothing and a little tar. I caused the girl to dress in the sailor's habit and to daub her face and hands with the tar. Then I conducted her to the boat and made her row, or appear to row at an oar. In the mean time, the Captain managed the escape of the father and mother. We sailed that night.

Seven days out, a French privateer chased us for three days and three nights but could not come up with us. We arrived in Baltimore, after a passage of fifteen days.

I did not tarry in port long, but shipped on board a brig bound to Turk's Island in the West-Indies for a cargo of salt. We sailed from Baltimore in Feb. 1803 and arrived there the 24th. of the same month.

The brig was so old and rotten that the mate informed the Captain that in his opinion she was unfit to take the cargo home. The Captain however disregarded the mate's advice and set sail the 27th. of March.

On that same day there arose a heavy gale which continued for two days, while the brig labored very much. The gale became quite moderate on the 29th.

Lost at Sea.

ON the 30th., I had the watch on deck from twelve o'clock until four in the afternoon. I took the helm from two until four. About half past three, I was standing very careless as the weather was quite moderate, when suddenly the tiller give me a blow on the side which hurt me considerably. However I made no complaint on account of my own carelessness.

Before many minutes had passed, I observed that when she pitched, she did not rise as usual. Although I feared something was the matter, I said nothing as yet. But continuing to observe the same thing, I called out to Mr. Cooper, the mate. I told him something was the matter with the brig.

"I see nothing the matter," he replied. He returned to his work, reducing the main-top-gallant-mast.

The Captain was asleep on the hen-coop. The remainder of the watch was sitting in the forecastle, mending some nets for the rigging.

The brig now made a pitch. The water came in upon her deck and it appeared she would never rise again.

I called again to Mr. Cooper and desired him to sound the pump. He flew into a passion at me. However he went to the pump and found five feet of water in the hold. He was then much frightened.

"All hands get out the long boat," he called.

We cut her lashings and put her overboard. The mate went into the cabin to get some provisions, but the water was so high that he could procure nothing but one bottle of spirits. We jumped into the boat having but one small sail made of a royal,

14

the ship's bread-bag which was in the boat and four oars.

There were five of us in the boat, the mate and four others. We called out to the Captain and remainder of the crew, eight in number. But to our great surprise, the brig made one plunge and never rose again. The last thing we saw was the Captain and two others running up the masthead.

It was difficult keeping the long boat from going down after the brig, in the convulsion of the water.

So we were left at the mercy of the waves, without a compass and with no food or water except two biscuit and one bottle of rum for five persons to subsist upon. We knew not which way to steer and saw no friendly sail for six days and nights.

On the seventh day, a vessel came alongside and took us in. The first thing they did was to give us some nourishment, milk and rum. The Captain was a sensible man and delt it out to us with great caution, lest we kill ourselves from over-eating. As soon as we were able to walk on deck, we kept up our cries for more victuals, which were not allowed to us, as we could not bear it.

But to return to our situation before we were taken up; our hunger was excessive and our thirst beyond any description. On the sixth day I fell asleep, was taken up in that condition, and did not know I had been saved for twelve hours after.

My first sensations upon waking were those of hunger. The Captain had tied my hands so that I might not get to the provisions and injur myself. So I observed where the cook put the meat after dinner. Accordingly I watched and as soon as the cabin was empty, I went to work on the victuals in the best manner I could with my hands tied. I had eaten but one or two mouthfulls when the Captain returned, finding me with my hands in the locker. He dragged me away and bound me to one of the stanchions in the cabin.

"You are welcome to all that is good for you," said he, "but you have not yet the discretion to feed yourself, your appetite is so voracious."

However I soon got about again and was landed in the West-Indies by this brig which was from Philadelphia. I got passage to Wilmington in North Carolina and then traveled to Baltimore.*

It will doubtless excite suprise that I did not return home after so long an absence from my friends.† However I was then young, rash and inconsiderate. I felt ambitious to retrieve my fortunes before I visited my friends, having lost all my property by the shipwreck.

* See note 8, page 94.
† Durand was seventeen years old at this time. He was only thirty-three when he wrote his narrative of his adventures.

The United States Navy Life in 1804, As Seen by An Enlisted Man

I NOW concluded I would no more venture to sea in small craft. A rendezvous had been opened in Baltimore, where men entered the United States service* for the frigate *John Adams* which was destined for the Mediterranean and the war against the Turks.

I entered on board this frigate for twelve $ per month. My old master received my advance, forty-eight $ and he furnished me with all the necessities for the intended voyage. I had four weeks' cruise on shore, before I boarded the tender to join the ship in New York. I went on board the frigate April 1, 1804.

Before I had been there long, I was stationed at the fore-top of the larboard watch as second captain. Here I was obliged to be more cautious than a private sailor, as I was responsible for the actions of my men during my station. But I pretty well knew my duty and always obeyed my commanders, although I did it more through fear than anything else.

* See note 9, page 95.

The midshipmen would aggravate the men so much that it would almost provoke any man to transgress all rule. Those who are unacquainted with the discipline of an armed ship will doubtless think it incredible that the inferior officers are allowed to use the sailors in a disgraceful manner.

Midshipmen who are mere boys* will not infrequently order a man to stoop so that they can beat him to advantage, if he happens to be taller than they. If the sailor make complaint to the superiors, they will doubtless order the master-at-arms to put the complainant in irons. If the Captain happen to be in a good humor when the report is made to him, the poor fellow may escape without severe punishment; but if the Captain be of a contrary humor, the prisoner is ordered to prepare himself and the boatswain to flog him unmercifully.

I have seen a man hauled up and made to receive eighteen lashes for a crime no more serious than spitting on the quarter deck. Such outrages on human nature ought not to be permitted by a government which boasts of liberty. No monarch in the world is more absolute than the Captain of a Man-of-war. The situation of a sailor, exposed as he is to the vicissitudes of life, to the inclemencies of the seasons, to the fury of storms and tempests,

* See note 10, page 99.

18

is sufficiently arduous without its being rendered more so by the cruelties of his fellow beings.

We sailed from New York, April 25th. 1804 bound for the Mediterranean to fight the Tripolitans. We took along with us ten gun boats, each mounting two long 32 pounders, except boats No. 2 and No. 9 which mounted but one each. We had a very pleasant passage until we came to the Western Isles, where we were becalmed. One day when the sea was smooth, we discovered a turtle not far off.

Accordingly we lowered a boat and went in pursuit of it. Before we returned, we caught 17. The Captain was much pleased and made our boat's crew a present of one of them. It was a sufficient repast for nine men.

However we touched at no place until we came to Gibraltar. Here the gunboats mounted the guns which they had carried in their holds. We took provisions on board and sailed for Malta, which is said to be 1100 miles up the straits from Gibraltar. We went into Sadacroix in the island of Sicily where we victualed and watered our ship and the whole fleet did the same. Then we sailed for Tripoli.

It so happened that we spoke with the United States frigate *President* coming down the straits. She informed us of a treaty between the United

States and Tripoli.* On board her were the crew of the *Philadelphia,* who had been redeemed from a horrid slavery of eighteen months.

We then cruised about for several days to see if any further disturbance would take place, but all was quiet. So we put back to Sadacroix and there I went on board the *Enterprise* schooner. Then we set sail for Tripoli. The Captain opened his orders, which were to proceed up the straits as far as Egypt and Jerusalem. I will sketch these places as briefly as possible.

Geography à la mode.

FROM March to November, the heat in Egypt is almost unsupportable to Europeans. Natives call the southerly winds poisonous; they are of such extreme heat that no animal body exposed to them can withstand their fatal influence. When such a wind exceeds three days blowing, the plague it brings becomes an epidemic. It commences when the Nile begins to fall and lessens when the Nile rises again.

Ophthalmia, dysentary, leprosy, dropsy &c. are the diseases common to the Egyptians.

The fertility of Egypt is well known to arise from the annual overflowing of the Nile. At first, no notice is taken of the rise of the river. About

* See note 11, page 100.

the end of June it has usually swelled to five or six cubits above its former standard. This is publicly proclaimed through the streets of Cairo by a crier and the daily increase continues to be proclaimed until the river attains the height of 16 peeks. Then great rejoicings are made and the inhabitants cry "Wassah Allah," which means "God hath given abundance."

Among the greatest curiosities of the country if not of the world, we must reckon the people called Psylli, who have the faculty, either natural or acquired, of enchanting the most venomous serpents, so that they have no power to bite. Mr. Bruce assures us that he saw a fellow eat a living serpent beginning with the tail and proceeding all the way up to its head, without the creature offering to resent so violent an injury.

The mummy pits, so called because they contain the embalmed bodies of ancient Egyptians, are subterraneous vaults of prodigious extent; but the art of preparing the bodies is now lost. It is said that some of the bodies thus enbalmed are perfect and distinct to this day, although immured as much as 300 years ago.

On Easter holidays, the Christians of Cairo practice a holy cheat by pretending that the bodies of the dead arise from the graves and then peacefully return to their places. Another of their favorite practices is teaching young camels to dance. The young camels are placed upon a heated floor with attending music. Then, by increasing the heat, the Christians create in the camels such uneasiness that they begin to move to the music. The music is suited to their step and, in this way, the camels learn to follow it without further heat or torture.

Babylon, founded by King Cambyses, stood on the site of this city. Sayd, on the West bank of the Nile, is said to be the ancient Egyptian Thebes. Suez, formerly a place of great trade, is now a small city. The harbor is poor; a ship of 22 guns cannot approach within three miles of the town. The nearest good water is the Well of Moses, twelve miles from the town.

From the inland regions of Africa, Egypt receives ivory, gold dust, gums and slaves.

The situation of a slave in Egypt is very much superior to the lot of those in the U. States. The Egyptian slave is a favorite family domestic and often rises to positions of rank and dignity.

From Egypt we went to Malta. This island was formerly called Melita and is situated in 15 deg. east long. and 44 north, 60 miles south of Cape Passaro in Sicily. The island is an oval figure, about five miles in circumference. It is supposed to contain about 60,000 inhabitants.

This island was given to the Knights of St. John in 1530 by Emperor Charles V, when the Turks drove them out of Rhodes. The Knights are an assembly of the Masonic order. When the Great Master dies, they permit no vessel to go out of the harbor until a new master is elected. They do this to prevent the Pope from interfering with the election.

The short sketch I have given of the island must satisfy the reader as I am now called on to proceed to Sadacroix, a very fine harbor and a considerable trading town, situated opposite Malta and about 60 miles distant. On my arrival there, I returned to my old ship, the frigate *John Adams*.

We sailed for Tripoli. There we tarried for some days, but found things most quiet. Then we came down the straits and joined our fleet at Malta.

There we victualed and watered the whole fleet and sailed for Tunis, which place we blockaded for several weeks.

I was drafted on board the *Constitution*.

The United States Man-of-War Constitution.

To my dissatisfaction, I found very different treatment on board her than that which I had experienced on the *John Adams*. The *Constitution* was commanded by Commodore Rodgers* and his first

* See note 12, page 100.

lieutenant, Mr. Blake, I am sorry to say but I must keep up the truth of my narrative, was cashiered out of the English service.

By coming to the United States this Mr. Blake initiated himself into the American service by throwing around a little money and a few high-sounding words. Accordingly he had been entered on board as First Lieutenant. He thought to cut as many capers and exercise as much power as his tyrannical disposition could suggest to him.

The old rat, however, was soon caught in his own tricks. His treatment of the crew was so ill, that it is with the greatest delicacy I attempt to detail a few of his outrages. First of all, as soon as I went on board, I was mustered and stationed in the fore-top of the starboard watch. The ship was much larger than the one I was accustomed to, therefore I did not know where my station was.

Lieutenant Blake ordered the boatswain's mate to apply the lash to me. Then, thinking the man did not strike me hard enough to satisfy his own hellish disposition, the Lieutenant must needs fall to himself and flog me until he was weary. That was his practice on all occasions.

Soon after, the sailors found out the history of this run-a-way British villain and we made a general protest before the Captain, saying that we would not serve under him any longer and petitioning the Captain to give us another officer.

I was now pretty smart and active and was accordingly made boatswain over the ship's boys. The custom is this: one boy is master over all the rest and when any boy is to be flogged, the master does it, instead of the boatswain's mate of the ship, who flogs the crew. I do not mention my appointment by way of boasting, because it is the most disagreeable duty that I was ever called upon to perform.

I shall here mention a circumstance that happened while I was on duty as boatswain. One morning this Mr. Blake came on deck and saw one of the boy's trowsers lying there. The boy had gone below to get a brush to scrub them.

"Get the cat," ordered this renagado lieutenant. When I fetched it, he told me to give the poor boy five dozen lashes.

Then, because he thought I did not strike hard enough, he snatched the cat out of my hand and struck me as hard as possible and then flogged the boy most cruelly.

Our blockading fleet consisted of nine sail besides nine gunboats. Our fleet was:

Constitution, 44 guns; *Essex,* 44 guns; *John Adams,* 36 guns; *Congress,* 38 guns; brigs *Siren,* 18 guns; *Argus,* 18 guns; *Vixen,* 12 guns;

Schooners *Enterprise,* 12 guns and *Nautilus,* 12 guns; Total, 9 sail.

Negociations now took place between our commander and the Tunisians. After the Tripolitans had made peace, the Tunisians thought themselves smart in making a disturbance, but we quickly brought them to terms as I have stated. Once a brig attempted to run by us into the port, trailed by our brig *Vixen,* but out of reach of the *Vixen's* guns.

Commodore Rodgers ordered us to clear and to get ready two brass pieces which we had captured from the Turks and which would throw shot a great distance. We hastily mounted them on the fore-castle of the *Constitution* and brought one of them to bear on the brig. So we brought her to very quick.

Nothing in particular took place that is worth mentioning, except a court martial which we held on the *Constitution.* They tried John Graves, captain of the main-top of the ship, for desertion. He was sentenced to receive three hundred lashes along side of the ships or be "whipped through the fleet" as they call it.

We now sailed for Malta and then to Sadacroix, where we stripped the *Constitution* of her sail and rigging and built a gig boat. For three months we tarried there, doing various kinds of work in the navy yard. I was five times innoculated for the small pox but as often it failed to have the desired effect.

At length, we sailed to Palermo, where an English fleet was lying at anchor. Here I saw some members of their crews flogged through the fleet, as had been done with the captain of our main-top. They were followed by musicians as they were taken from ship to ship. At the end of this punishment they were put under hospital treatment until they were again capable of duty, if indeed they survived the flogging, which they seldom did.

We went to Algiers. Here the Dey gave us a feast. There was nothing these Turks would not do for us, since we had bottled up the ports at Tunis and Tripoli. The feast consisted of beef, mutton and various fresh meats and vegetables, enough for all our crew of 450 men and with an abundance left over. The Dey came on board us, to make his compliments to Commodore Rodgers. He brought his retinue of attendants with him and was very splendidly entertained by our commander for four or five hours.

When he approached alongside, a salute was fired, every yard was manned and every one of the crew was dressed all in white. When he returned to shore, another salute was fired and our commander accompanied him.

Nothing else transpired here, except a ludicrous accident which befell me alone. One day when I was on shore, I chanced to meet a Turkish woman, dressed in black with a white muffler on. Nothing could be seen but her eyes. The novelty of her dress, coupled with the strange appearance of the streets which are covered overhead, threw me into a strange suprise. So that I, although I was a stout-hearted tar, ran all the way back to the place where I had left the boat's crew. Then I fully informed myself about their customs of dress.

Learning is at a low ebb in this country. Some of the governors are unable to write their own names. The people have manners like the Egyptians. They subsist by piracy. They are bold and enterprising in their attacks and will fight desperately to obtain a prize at sea. However, they are much inferior to Europeans in the construction and management of their ships.

I shall conclude the subject of Algerian customs by making some remarks about their treatment of Christian captives. They are wholly destitute of humanity and when any Christian has fallen into their power, he is taken to a market and sold to the highest bidder. Then too, he is often bastinadoed by his captors, to make him tell the condition of his property in his native land, for the Algerians love to make their captives buy their liberty by paying a ransom. Few captives survive the hardships imposed upon them for any length of time.

After three weeks in Algiers, there came on board a Turkish ambassador and we carried him to Sardinia, where we landed him. There, in the harbor of Calleroy, I saw an excellent row galley, with a keel 162 feet long. These gallies never carry any sail but are propelled by ninety to a hundred oars or sweeps. These are exercised or pulled by Christian captives. The captives are chained to the oars and their taskmasters apply supple jack to their naked bodies at every failure or inability to obey orders. They suffer everything that man can suggest to render them more miserable. Their pitiable condition I shall remember as long as my memory lives.

After cruising about, we came to Cadiz, where the whole Spanish and French fleet lay. At the mouth of the harbor Lord Nelson was lying with 27 English sail of the line. The French and Spanish fleet consisted of 33 sail.

The British, seeing us make for the harbor, made sail after us. But our old *Constitution* showed them her stern. We entered the harbor and came to anchor. I belonged to the first lieutenant's boat and so had an opportunity to go aboard several French men-of-war as he went about the fleet. At

length, our officers went to a ball upon a French
74, called the *Neptune*.

An Exchange of Officers.

ON the 19th. day of October, 1805, we put to sea,
but having little wind, did not get far from land.
At day light, we found ourselves close in to the
British fleet. Signals were given from the Admiral's ship to give us chase and soon one of their
sail came within hail.

"What ship are you?"

"U.S. frigate *Constitution*."

"Where from?"

"Cadiz."

"Then," came the reply, "I'll send my boat on
board."

So their captain came on board and, after hold-
ing some conversation with Commander Rodgers,
sailed directly back to the British admiral. The
admiral immediately made signal for the whole
fleet to close and to stand a little out to sea.

On the 21st. the combined fleets really got out of
the harbor to attack the English. We supposed
that the action started about 9 o'clock, when we
were ten miles off. We could not see them long, but
their cannon made a tremendous thunder.* We

* See note 13, page 100.

proceeded on to Gibraltar, where we gave the information that the combined fleets were really engaging the English fleet. After a visit to Sadacroix and Malta, we returned to Gibraltar.

Commodore Rodgers went on board the frigate *Essex*, and the tyrannical lieutenant Mr. Blake, before mentioned, was exchanged for a first lieutenant named Ludlow, who had belonged to the *Essex*. Captain Campbell took command of the *Constitution* to my great satisfaction.

Under orders from our government, the *Essex* now sailed for home. The gun boats accompanied her to America. I had been in the U. States' service for one year and ten months and had only two months more service to make up the term of my enlistment. Had I been permitted to return on the *Essex*, that term would have expired by the time I reached New York. Instead of this, I was obliged to stay on the *Constitution* and made a second round of the straits. We sailed up the straits to Algiers, Malta and Tunis. At this last port, we stayed some time, as our Captain had considerable business to transact for the government. I nearly lost my life there, when a heavy sea washed me overboard. However I caught a rope, when twenty-feet astern and made it fast around my middle. I was hauled out but the rope was so small that it cut me and I could not return to duty for some time.

On our passage to Malta, we experienced a heavy gale of wind. We came out of Tunis in very agreeable weather, with every sail set, but the ship was struck by what we call a Levant wind, which almost upset her. We had just time to take in our studding sails and royals, and attempted to get down our top-gallant yards. But it was all in vain. The gale was so violent that it was impossible.

Sailing Master Baggot came forward with two bottles of rum which he offered to any man who would go to the mast head and cut the top gallant yards away. Many of the sailors wished for the rum, but no one dared attempt it. We hauled our mainsail up to the yard, but could not hand it. It blew all to pieces. It was five o'clock in the afternoon and the gale continued until nine in the morning.

Our main sail was sprung astern three times, the length of the ship. We repaired our ship in Malta. The damages in cost amounted to 500 $.

At Sadacroix, we remained some time. The officers took their pleasure on shore while the men stayed hard at work on board, greatly abused and hindered by the younger officers.

The Mutiny on the Constitution.

ONE Sunday, all hands were called to go into the water to wash. One of the men swam as far as the

32

ship's buoy. A lieutenant called to him to return, but the noise of the water prevented the sailor hearing the command. The lieutenant then ordered someone to swim out and tell him to come aboard, which he did immediately he heard the order.

"Strip," ordered the lieutenant, as soon as he came on deck.

Having nothing on but a thin cotton shirt, the man refused.

At which Lieutenant Burroughs seized a hand-spike and struck at him with all his might. The sailor dexterously avoided the blow, which would have caused his death. This produced an alarm among us, for we said that the man should not be punished.*

Mr. Burroughs then went up on the quarter deck and ordered the marines to fire upon us, but they refused. So the officers got their swords and pistols and stood guard on us themselves. They now piped down the hammocks and ordered every man to bed. We obeyed them.

Then they sent for the Captain who was at Cutania, a town seven miles away from the ship. He came up the side of the ship in great haste, but being a man of noble mind, proceeded to inquire into the matter with great regularity. In spite of the fact that he had heard only the officers' side of

* See note 14, page 101.

33

the matter in their message, he looked hard at the lieutenant when he found him in arms on the deck.

"Follow me to my cabin," he ordered, "I fear me there is some misconduct among the officers as well as among the crew."

After a short stay in his cabin, he caused the purser to come up into his quarters and to make out a ship's list of every man in service; those whose enlistments had expired in one roll and those who still owed service in another roll. This was done according to order. The next morning at 8 o'clock, the captain called all hands to the quarter deck and directed those whose times were out to remain.

"Now," said the Captain, "state your grievances."

So the armorer of the ship, whose name was Shoemaker, related every circumstance of abuse we had suffered during the Captain's absence, stating that men had been flogged six months after their time of service had expired. They informed him that they would be happy to proceed to America quietly under his command, if he would give the order to sail at once. Otherwise they would take command of the ship themselves and conduct her thither.

"Well," said the Captain, "if you have a mind to take the ship, you may. But if you will wait until I can settle my business, I will sail for America and make the voyage as quick as possible and from now on, no man shall be punished unless he deserves it."

At this time, there were three men in irons. They were the man who was ordered to pull off his shirt to be flogged, the boatswain's mate who refused to flog him and another man who said he should not be flogged. They were kept in irons until we reached America, where, as I have since heard, they recovered some hundred dollars damages.

The Captain hurried to despatch his business. We came to Messina. As the Captain was about to go on shore, he ordered the top-gallant-yards to be sent down. The men would not obey, saying that they were homeward bound and that home they would go. So the Captain did his business without making them comply.

Six days later, we came to Naples. There are said to be not less than 300 lawyers in Naples. At first I thought this a great exaggeration, but according to the best information I could obtain, it was the case.

From Naples, we went to Leghorn where we took on board some marble, which was to be used for erecting a monument to the illustrious Washington. We stopped at Salamanca where bull fights are exhibited for three days in the public square in the month of June, each year. The officers had a ball here.

At Malaga we heard of the action between the United States frigate *Chesapeake* and the British 50 gun ship *Leopard*.* In consequence of this and of spreading rumors, our Captain supposed that war had taken place between the two countries.

Homeward Bound.

WE had then only 44 guns mounted. Our Captain called all hands on deck and asked us if we would fight our way to America, if he mounted four more guns. We answered him in the affirmative with three hearty cheers. Accordingly we went to work, mounted four more guns and got ready for sea after eight days in port.

Because of the supposed war with England, our Captain ran past the port of Gibraltar and into the harbor of Algeziras. Then he sent a boat into Gibraltar to get information about the war. The boat crew found that in Gibraltar they knew nothing about it.

On the same day, the American sloop of war, *Wasp*, came in through the gut of Gibraltar. Our Captain made signal for her to anchor alongside, which she did. She had orders for us to proceed to America as soon as possible. We sent the *Wasp* to Malaga for provisions and water. She returned in two days.

* See note 15, page 101.

So we now set sail for Boston, after being up the Mediterranean two years and nine months. We had a tolerable good passage and in 45 days arrived off Boston light house, on the 5th of December 1806.

We lay in Boston for twelve days and then received orders to go to New York to be paid off. During this time I belonged to the boat party, but I cannot say I thought myself under actual hire as my enlistment had long since expired. But I hoped to receive my pay for past services, over and above the term of my enlistment also I was not willing to be counted in any way disorderly or mutinous. So I continued to do duty.

One evening our officers went ashore to a ball. I belonged to the boat that took them thither. We were under the command of a midshipman who had orders to wait for the party until a certain hour in the evening. Since the officers did not arrive at that hour, we thought to go back on the frigate, but the midshipman said he would stay as long as he thought proper.

It was very cold and, as the boat was along side the wharf, we asked permission to go up on the wharf and exercise to make ourselves warm. The midshipman granted this.

The officers not returning, the midshipman called to us to come in the boat and take him on board. I did not hear his first call and for this reason exasperated him greatly. As soon as we were on board the frigate, the midshipman made complaint to the Master of the *Constitution* who was his brother.

The Master, without asking or hearing my defense, give me twelve stripes as hard as he could strike with a three inch rope, which sorely bruised me.

I considered myself my own man, as the term of my enlistment had been up these eight or nine months. Therefore I put on what clothing I could wear that belonged to me and quitted the ship. I have not seen the officers since nor as yet received any pay for my services up the Mediterranean, which pay amounts to more than 350 $.

I must here ask the reader the propriety of making small boys, 10 to 12 years of age, officers and giving them full authority to flog and abuse the men, when they are as yet unacquainted with the actual duty belonging to a ship. I have known them to give orders which were executed according to their command, but which proved wrong, when reviewed by an older officer. Then I have heard the midshipmen deny having given the order in question and the men who obeyed them faithfully were flogged for it.

A Voyage to France on a
Blockade Runner

AFTER I left the boat and went on shore, I
found myself not only unacquainted with the
place but also without friends or money. I procured some refreshment at a house and walked over
Charlestown bridge where I took lodgings for the
night. Here I met a sailor who asked me to what
ship I belonged.

"I served up the Mediterranean on the U. States
Essex and the *Constitution*," I replied, "but I've
left her on account of ill usage. So I have resolved
to go to New York by some other means and wait
for the *Constitution* to arrive there, so that I can
be paid off."

He told me of a brig, bound for France, which
was to stop in New York. He said that this brig
was needing a hand. I accordingly shipped on the
brig with the understanding that I would be permitted freedom to leave her in New York for a few
hours so that I could collect the money due me.

No sooner were we out of port than a gale of
wind arose which blew us out to sea. The first port
we made was Bellisle in France. From Boston to
Bellisle was a passage of twenty-five days. We ar-

rived there January 27th. 1807. Our true port was Nantz.

On the morning after our arrival at Bellisle, we hired a pilot to conduct us to Nantz, forty miles away. We got under way about 9 o'clock in the morning and as it was very foggy it was a fine time to escape. The British were blockading the ports of France.

However, in spite of the fog, we had not sailed far when we saw a British 74 in chase of us. She cut us off from the land, so that we could not get into Nantz, but were forced to anchor at a place called Goree, about 60 miles from Nantz. Therefore we discharged our cargo there and sent it to Nantz in waggons. This was a considerable trouble as our cargo was sugar, mollasses, cotton, boxwood &c.

While we were lying at Goree, two men-of-war were launched there and General Napoleon himself came to the launching.

He had on a snuff-colored coat and breeches, very indifferent hat and epauletts and I could observe no marks of haughtiness about his person. The most I can say of him is that he is small in stature, dark complexion, but has a sharp and expressive countenance.

We all attended meeting or service in the forepart of the day on Sundays, while we were in this place and danced in the latter part, for Sunday is the greatest day for amusement of any day in the whole week. Provisions in Goree are very cheap. A man may go on shore and have as good an entertainment as he might wish for one French crown or five shillings, lawful money.

When we had unladen our ship, we took in ballast which was brought to our ship's side as small pebbles. It was carried by women in baskets, which they balanced on their heads. They emptied it down the hatchway. Our Captain sold his cargo for money and, at that time, it was unlawful to take money out of the country. Accordingly it was smuggled on board in small quantities at night. Each man brought his share on board in a belt that was strapped around his middle. Each belt held about 100 crowns.

Our design was, as soon as we got ready, we would go to the West-Indies for a cargo of salt, but the English prevented us. We came out of the harbor about 5 o'clock, leaving Bellisle about 7 o'clock P.M. On the following morning about daylight, we found a British ship astern of us with all sail set.

Captured by the English.

WE advised Captain Pick to also set all his sail but he would not follow our judgement. So the British ship *Shannon* soon came up to us. They gave us a shot and we hove to. They sent their boat with a lieutenant on board. He overhauled us, then told us to make sail.

However we had not sailed far before they fired at us again. They came on board a second time and ordered us to make ready to go on board the *Shannon* as prisoners. Every man had his belt full of gold and silver and the money for the cargo which we could not put into our belts, we secreted, so that it would not be found if searched for.

We packed up our things and boarded them. They did not leave one man from our crew on board the brig. They took us to Plymouth in England, where we remained as prisoners for six weeks. We were on a very short food allowance, scarcely sufficient to sustain life. The first sustenance I received on board them was some boiled oat-meal without salt or butter or other seasoning. In America we ordinarily feed our swine better than this, but I was obliged to eat it to preserve life.

At Plymouth, we were finally allowanced. This allowance consisted of nine pounds of pork, half a pint of pease, one pound of bread (fourteen ounces to the pound) for six men for two days. Six of our men were allowed no more than four of theirs. We lived in this manner for six weeks.

I made myself as happy as I could and used to

sport with the ship's company, because in this way I got more to eat. I had seventy crowns upon me, which was not discovered. At the end of six weeks, we fell in with the Channel Fleet and were put on board the *Ville-de-Paris* of 110 guns and sent to Torbay at the town of Bricksom. I considered myself happy to get there. We then got passage to Plymouth, to join our brig once more.

On our arrival, we found that the English had eaten all the provisions on the brig. We procured some through the assistance of the Consul. Our Captain Pick left us to go to London to try to clear the brig. He was absent for near three months, before we heard from him. In fact, he never returned to the brig, when he found he could not clear her for she had been condemned as a runner.

So we were turned out on shore, having spent our money and sold our clothes for our support during the time we waited on the brig. We applied to the Consul, but he would allow us only a shilling a day each, which was enough to buy but one meal.

As no American vessels were going out of port, I shipped on a Swedish vessel to go to Portsmouth, thinking that I could get passage from there to America. I hired for 15 $ per month. The Swedish captain died of a sickness before we reached Portsmouth.

Now lying in this harbor was a brig belonging

to New York. I applied to the Captain for a passage but was refused. I then informed the Consul of this circumstance, who wrote a letter to the brig's Captain which made the latter very indignant against me. However he told me to bring my things on board Friday. This was a Wednesday. The Captain informed me he would come to anchor at Spithead. On my arrival there, I found that they had put off without me. I was obliged to put back to the town and pay the waterman 10s.

You may judge if my feelings were very pleasant when I found that I was stranded again with very little money and no employment. I put up for the night at Mr. Turner's and there I met an English transport officer, who had heard good reports of me from the pilot of the Swedish vessel. He was in want of a mate and offered me a situation.

"I am afraid of being impressed by the British," I told him.

"I can protect you from capture by the press gang," he replied.

I knew nothing else to do for a livelyhood, so I shipped as mate with him for seven pounds per month.

In the month of March 1809 we took a hundred and forty-nine prisoners on board and sailed for Spain under convoy of two gun brigs from Plymouth. Then we joined other sail to the number of

44

forty. After the fifth day out, thick fogs caused the fleet to separate and some of the vessels put in at one place and some at another. However, after being out eighteen days we made land and found that we were 30 miles to leeward of Corunna, our intended harbor.

The wind and currents were so unfavorable that we were forced to beat on and off for three days. At last, the prisoners got discouraged, took the brig from us and put her into Vevarrow Bay. They hoisted themselves a boat or boats, put themselves and what they wished into them and took themselves and our property off. It would have been folly for us to tempt resistance as we were seven in number and they were 149 against us.

As I was mate of the brig, I was forced to make an accounting of all the blankets, sheets and pilows that were in her before the prisoners decamped. After the prisoners left us, we put things in order on board and in three days came to Corunna. The greatest part of the fleet, under convoy, lay in the harbor. We remained here for three months with little to do.

I had saved some money, over and above our wages, by supplying the cook with a morning bitter each day. Accordingly the cook gave me all the slush or fat that remained after cooking. This thing is allowed all cooks on shipboard for themselves. So on our passage I secured 95 pounds and sold it very high in Corunna.

We waited, as I said, for three months to take on board some British troops that were in Spain and sailed July 10th., 1809 for Plymouth, where we arrived after a passage of 21 days. As soon as we came to anchor, I went on shore for a short time and then returned on board.

Impressed into the British Navy

AT length we were ordered out to sea. The men wished for a little pleasure on shore before we sailed and asked the Captain for permission.

"I have no objections," he said, "but there is a very hot press on shore and you'll all do better to stay on board."

This caution had no effect on the plans of the men and they accordingly went. I was afraid of the press and stayed on board.

While they were away, about 11 o'clock at night, there came along side a boat belonging to the *Narcissus* frigate. They boarded our brig and they came below where I was asleep. With much abuse, they hauled me out of my bed, not suffering me to even put on or take anything except my trowsers.

In this miserable condition, I was taken on board their ship but did not think to be detained there for a term of seven years. Had I known my destiny that night, I would have instantly committed the horrid crime of self-murder. In this sorrowful condition I spent the night. At day light, I found my way on deck and soon after heard the word given to un-moor the ship and get her ready for sea.

At this, I was overcome by grief. I ran below and tried to procure some paper, pen and ink from the members of the crew, offering any price. I was able to offer money, as I had concealed some of my savings by tying the coins in a handkerchief about my neck. The robbers who took my money from my belt did not find this horde. However no member of the crew durst sell me pen, ink nor paper, as they guessed my intention of writing for aid to escape from a hateful service.

There came along side a boat with stuff to sell. For a shilling, I procured a sheet of paper on which I wrote a letter to the Captain of the brig. I desired him to break open my chest and take out my protection and indenture and send them on board as quick as possible. I hired the boat to take this message to him immediately. The message boat made all possible speed; she had a mile and one-half to go, yet she went with such rapidity that in one hour and one-half after, the Captain was on board with my indenture and protection.

The Lieutenant of the *Narcissus* said he could do nothing about clearing me, but told the Captain of the brig that if he (the Captain) would go ashore and see the Captain of the frigate, he would direct him where to find him.

There is an island to pass, between the spot where we lay on the frigate and the town. It is called Drake's Island. It was my bad fortune that the Captain of the brig carrying my protection and indenture passed on one side of this isle in the message boat, while the Captain of the *Narcissus* passed it on the other side. Therefore they missed each other and my last chance of regaining my liberty was gone. As soon as our Captain arrived on the *Narcissus*, he weighed anchor and put out to sea. I never saw the Captain of the brig again.

In this unfortunate manner, I was dragged on board a British man-of-war, August 21st. 1809. Despair so complete seized my mind, that I lost all relish for the world. For the first twelve days thereafter, my entire victualing would not have amounted to the one ration as it was allowed us.

I lost, as I left behind me on the brig, more than 50 pounds sterling, a chest full of excellent and well-chosen clothes. Only lately I had quitted the service of the U. States' after enduring everything. The thought of serving with the British fleet touched every nerve with distress and almost deprived me of reason. I had been eight years from home and I began to despair of ever seeing that place again.

After I had been on board a few days, the Captain called me to the quarter deck and asked me if I would enter. He said that if I would, he would give me 5 pounds.

I utterly refused, telling him I was an American. I also said I would not do duty if I could help it.

"If you will not work I'll flog you until you're glad to set about it," said the Captain. "Go below, for I won't hear another word out of you."

Below decks, I found twelve more Americans who had been previously impressed. One of them told me that, when he refused to obey an order, the Captain had given him four dozen lashes. "Therefore," said he to me, "I advise you to do as you are bid."

I thought this excellent advice and I went to work and made myself as contented as possible. I concluded I would write to the American consul when we came to port again.

We voyaged to France and lay to off the port of Nantz. Near us lay the *Shannon*, on which I was detained a prisoner when they took the American brig as a prize. Some of the *Shannon's* crew told me I had better have stayed with them.

"Our Captain is twice as clever as the Captain of the *Narcissus*," they said.

"Yes," I replied, "I'd give the devil one if he'd take the other."

At length, I was noticed by our Captain and put in the gig boat. Our allowance for food was so small that I began to lose flesh. One night the gig boat was ordered to go thirty miles from the ship under cover of the darkness, to a place called Horse Island. This lies about 4 miles from the main land. A great many small boats come out there to pass it by, and our purpose was to capture them.

The island was uninhabited except for five wild horses we saw there. We had only two days provisions with us and, as we stayed there five days, we were forced to shoot one of the horses for food. Neither did we durst make much fire, through fear of being seen from the main land and being surprised and captured. However we made a little fire that just scorched the outside of the meat, which we ate with a great relish, notwithstanding that we had no salt to put on it.

We returned to the frigate after the fifth day on the island. We were not put on duty the morning we returned, which we considered a great favor. The next day again, we were sent off in the same boat, to try if our luck would be better.

This time we took five prizes and brought them to the frigate. They were full of stores and supplies for General Napoleon. They were small craft, called "chamois," of five to 25 tons burden.

Our Captain, considering my forwardness in taking and securing these boats, gave me better usage than I had previously received.* We lay off Nantz for six months, then returned to Plymouth.

* See note 16, page 108.

At once I wrote to our Consul at London, but I have since then been informed that my letters as well as those of other impressed Americans, were intercepted. Even the petitions which the Consul made were little noticed and many a sailor brought himself to an untimely end through despair, in consequence of this cruelty and oppression which is called British courage and justice.

We were informed that the French fleet had escaped from Brest. We were ordered to Barbadoes with despatches to inform Admiral Cochrane of their escape.

In the West-Indies Again as a British Sailor.

On our way we captured a French merchantman which was bound for Martinico. These are the particulars of it. Eighteen days out from Brest, early one morning, we espied a sail upon our weather, standing with the wind in her starboard quarter. She was about two leagues distant, with her studding sails set. We gave chase, but since we had the wind directly aft, we hauled our wind on the starboard tack and took in our leeward studding sails.

Soon after we came within gun shot. We gave her a bow shot to the windward, to bring her to, but she still stood on her course. Then we hauled a little to the wind and gave her several shots until at length we shot away her main-top-mast, at which she hove to. When we came within pistol shot, we put out our boat and brought her crew on board. She was a brig, richly laden with cordage and provisions and mounting one 21 pounder.

We put 18 men and a lieutenant on board her and ordered her to the Barbadoes. On the 25th day we arrived there ahead of our prize. We tarried but two hours, having learned that Martinico had surrendered to His Majesty's forces. We sailed for that port where we found the fleet riding out the bay of Port Royal. We delivered the despatches to the Admiral and watered ship.

Next the *Narcissus* was ordered to cruise to the windward, keeping out a sharp look for the French fleet which had escaped from Brest. On the third day, we discovered a French corvette making in for the island. We kept to the leeward of her for three days sailing, but when another sail came between her and the island, we were able to come within reach of shot.

Upwards of 100 shots were exchanged, before she struck her colors to us. She was a national corvette, mounting 22 guns. We put a prize master on board and sent her to St. Pierre. In the course of 12 days cruise, we had but one man killed and we made four prizes.

Then we returned to port to make ready to take

part in an expedition against the Saints, a small island lying about five leagues to the westward of Guadaloupe. From thence we were to proceed to Barbadoes to take in troops destined for the operation against the island.

We took transport ships under our convoy. They had 2,000 troops on board them, which force was to make the attack. We were obliged to land the men in flat bottomed boats, under cover of our cannon. We did this in the space of two hours.

One of our light vessels was sent up to keep the fort in play until the land attack could be formed. Our men took two mortar pieces on shore and planted them. While we were busy at this, three French sail of the line and two of their frigates slipped out and escaped us.

Then our land party under General Walter made a noble assault in every part of the island. They resisted us for ten hours then retired to the forts for safety. We kept up the siege for five days.

Wounded by a French Shot.

I was one of a party which, on the fifth morning, was making a breast works and platform on which we were to plant some more mortars. While working there, an 18 pound shot from them struck the planking next me and a splinter of it broke my leg just below the calf. I was taken to the surgeon's

54

tent, where a temporary dressing was put on then was sent to the cock-pit on board the *Narcissus,* where I underwent a more careful dressing of my hurt.

The following night, the forts surrendered. I never knew the conditions of the surrender. The British lost, in killed and wounded, more than 300 men. The islanders' loss was said to be more than 700. The wounded were all taken on board and after a common attendance with our own people, were received as prisoners of war.

I was allowed to be confined in a cot as the condition of my leg would not permit me to make use of a hammock. All I could do was to ruminate on the various incidents of my life and there was nothing to prevent these reflections but the pain of my leg. Therefore, like Hamlet, I reasoned with myself. I had been in the service of the British for more than a year and if I continued seven more, I decided I would see my limbs scattered all over the globe and like the wages promised me by the U. States' service, it would get me nothing material.

"If I kill or am killed," said I to myself, "who is there to benefit except King George?"

> *The world's a stately bark—*
> *On dangerous seas*
> *To be boarded at your peril,*

said I, with the poet.

In the meantime, we victualed, watered and got ready for sea in the harbor of Port Royal. Here they had some talk of sending me on shore; but through fear of my escape, they changed their minds and continued me on board.

We cruised for three weeks and made several attacks on a French frigate of superior metal, but as the weather was boisterous, we could not board her. On the last attempt, we were parted by a heavy gale just as the sun went down. In the morning the French frigate had either gone down in the storm or made her escape.

They did us so much damage with their shot between wind and water and with balls which carried a part of our rigging away that we were obliged to go into port to repair the damages.

During this battle, I lay on my cot in an extraordinary uneasyness, wishing to fight rather than to have our colors strike but more because of bravado and pride than because of any self interest in the outcome. But the thought of lying there still while there was so much thunder overhead was, at the same time, insupportable to me. Had not the surgeon's attendants kept me in, I would have stood at my gun and served it.

However, after the affray was over, when the surgeon examined all the wounded, he found my leg still inflamed. He conceived that all was not right. Therefore he measured and found my injured leg one inch shorter than the other. As a result, I was forced to bear the painful operation of having it broken all over again and newly set. In this condition I was slowly recovering for 60 days before I could be called a "tight sailor" as the saying is, or fit for duty.

Next we were ordered to England, after we had picked up two officers at St. Thomas who were being returned. We arrived in Plymouth July 17, 1810. Here we waited for six or seven weeks for repairs. I was not allowed to go on shore nor to converse with boats that came alongside. I was then put at the business of sail making.

Next we were sent to France to cruise off L'Orient. We found a French brig and schooner lying in Coneall Bay. The brig mounted 14 guns and had 150 men on board. Accordingly, we attempted to cut them out of the bay with our ship's boats. Five boats and fifty men were selected for this purpose.

We rowed five miles with the tide and came up near the French sail about 8 o'clock in the evening. They hailed us.

"Are you coming to pay us a visit?" they asked.

"Yes," was our answer and we gave them three cheers.

"Come along, we're ready," said they.

Our boats took their station, one on each quarter. The master's boat was in the center. We attempted to board the brig, but we met with every resistance, as they were fully prewarned against our attack.

As we came along side I attempted to board her by seizing hold of a small cannon whose muzzle protruded through an open port. Finding it impossible to get a footing at this point, I stepped back. I had no sooner done so than she discharged her whole contents at our boat.

Then I attempted to board her by seizing hold of the netting, but I was met by two of their men armed with boarding pikes. I drew a pistol and killed one of them on the spot. I could not reload, as I must keep one hand in the netting, so I killed the other with my second pistol. Then I attempted to board her, sword in hand, but was severely wounded in my leg.

After a while, I grew weak from the loss of blood and fell back into our boat. Two of our boats were destroyed, ten men killed and fifteen wounded. We retreated.

While they were rowing us away, a shot hit the stern of our boat. She took in water very fast and we would all have been drowned there, had not one of the men plugged the hole with the head of a dead man who had been killed at the discharge of the cannon.

With other wounded, I was sent to the hospital at Plymouth, where I was cared for 31 days. I applied for my discharge but it was refused me. My reputation for courage in a fight prevented my being discharged,* as it gained me interest from the officers, so that they would not suffer me to go.

The Captain was transferred to another ship and Captain Almyer took command. By his direction, I joined the musicians thinking it easier to play an instrument in the ship's band than to do ship's duty. There was a first rate instructor and for three weeks while we chased French privateers, my chief work was blowing on a flute. Gradually I gained some proficiency at it.

The Captain now purchased new instruments equal to a full band. I learned the claronet. Even this did not occupy my mind and I longed to return to my own home and my own country. One day, I asked for permission to go ashore. Captain Almyer refused me.

"For," said he, "you will escape and will be caught and flogged through the fleet."

Nevertheless, I resolved to escape but the guards were so plenty that I had no chance to put my design into execution. Then the fleet sailed for Spain.

* See note 17, page 109.

There were the frigates *Amazon, Dryad, Arathusa*
and *Narcissus*. We took on board some Spanish
troops whom we carried to St. Antony and landed
them there in spite of the French who had possession of the place. However there was later a battle
in which the French general was killed with a great
many of his men, but for all that, they chased the
Spanish troops up into the mountains and forced
us back on the ships.

The *Amazon*, a Spanish frigate and our *Narcissus* were ordered to Corunna. The wind was
ahead, so we put into Vevarrow Bay for the night.
The Spanish frigate anchored ahead of us. In the
night a great wind arose and she dragged her an-
chors. Then she drifted on our bow. Our rigging
was tangled and her fore-yards, our fore-mast and
main-mast all came down on the deck together.
Then she dropped astern of us and ran foul of a
Spanish brig, whose cable parted. They both ran
ashore and only 18 men from their crews of 750
men were saved. This was Nov. 21st, 1811.

On our ship, two men were killed and eighteen
injured by the falling of the masts. In the morning,
the crew of the *Amazon* came aboard us to help
repair the damage. We worked for four days and
then put to sea, to go to Plymouth to refit.

A tremendous storm came up. The wind tore
our sails to pieces. With every surf, we expected to

go to the bottom, as our stern was shattered by the falling masts. She took in a great deal of water and for days the wind blew the most violently I have ever experienced in many years service. Through God's mercy we were spared. So we put into Plymouth dock to repair.

A Trip on Shore after Three Years' Impressment.

WHEN a ship undergoes a careful repairing, it is customary to take off her deck, pull her down to the keel and build her up with new timbers. In such a case, it takes three to four months to refit. If the Captain has any influence with the Admiralty, he is allowed to retain his hands, instead of recruiting anew. To save them for him, they are sent aboard a hulk for quarters until the ship is again ready for sea. This was the case with us. Our stores, guns and supplies were taken out of the *Narcissus* and we went aboard a hulk while they repaired her.

I had now been three years in the service and I thought it high time to go on shore. I asked the Captain for permission and he said I might, if I would give him my promise not to make my escape. So I went with the musicians who had orders to watch me, although I did not know it at the time. I stayed on shore for 24 hours, enjoying every kind of diversion I thought proper, and then I returned to the hulk.

At that place, ships are built with great expedition. I saw a 74 gun ship launched from the stocks on June 21, 1812 and the same day hauled from her ways into a dry dock. On the 22nd. carpenters were employed coppering her bottom, on the 23rd. she came out of dock and was beside a sheer hulk where she took in her masts and bowsprit. Next she was hauled to the hulk where she was to be rigged. On the 24th. the shrouds were put over her mast-head and the dead eyes turned in, the lower rigging rattled down, fore and aft, her bowsprit shrouds and bob-stays put on, all three top masts pointed through and made ready for swaying away before 12 o'clock. Hands were then piped to dinner and turned up at 1 o'clock. The top masts were swayed, their rigging set up, the fore-castle men rigged, their jib and flying-jib boom after guard, the spanker boom sent up, the fore and main yard and top-sail yards were sent up.

While some of the men were bending the fore and main sail, the fore, main and mizzen-top sails were bent; main-top-mast and middle and top-gallant stay sails bent; jib and spanker bent; mizzen-stay-sail, top sails, top gallant halyards rove, fore and main braces rove; likewise all the running rigging that was necessary. All this was done by sun set. On the 25th. one-half the ship's company was employed on one side of the ship taking on guns, while the other half, on the other side, the larboard, were taking in provisions, stores and water.

On the 26th. she was complete and ready for sea and on the 28th. of the same month, she joined the Channel fleet. To explain the manner in which they rig a ship so quickly, the reader will understand that the rigging is already fitted in the dock yard, before the ship is launched. All they have to do is put it in a lighter, bring it alongside and put it in its place.

I must here make mention of our crew which our Captain was so loath to part with; he applied to the admiralty and got a grant to keep them in the temporary hulk for three months, expecting that his ship would be over-hauled and ready to sail at the end of that time. However, the ship carpenters found her hull so rotten that she was obliged to undergo six months repairs. The crew was accordingly drafted.

It is a courtesy that is always extended to Captains to allow them to keep their own boat's crew. When our crew was drafted away, the Captain chose to keep the band instead. So we were sent aboard the *St. Salvadore*, a guard ship, to await his pleasure. Now she had been a Spanish ship of

120 guns which the British had captured. She had on board 1750 men, including prisoners. Here we were to tarry, I mean the band, until our Captain was ready for sea. I went on board this ship March 7th. 1812 and left her February 19, 1813.

Our Captain came on board and ordered that we of the band of music were to have as much liberty on shore as possible. But that was an insufficient sop to my feelings. Daily the cruelty I saw inflicted upon poor Americans was enough to fill the worst heart with horror.

There was a court martial held on board, May 9, 1812. Two Englishmen and an American were tried. The crime alleged was desertion. After what passed for a trial, the sentences were pronounced. Each Englishman was to receive 250 lashes and the American was to receive 300. They were to be whipped through the fleet.

Three days later, the sentence was carried out. A large boat came alongside, with a gallows erected on her. The poor prisoners were fastened to this, naked from the waist up. All the time the music played the rogues' march.

After the sentence had been read by the Captain, the boatswain's mate was ordered to proceed with the flogging. The American, whose name was Armstrong, first received 25 lashes and then each

64

of the Englishmen received 18. This was repeated beside each ship, with the music playing.

As John Armstrong was alongside the last ship, he expired under the brutality of the punishment. So they give his body ten lashes after he had died. His corpse was carried to the hospital and the doctors gave it as their opinion that some blood vessel broke inwardly and caused his death. The two Englishmen recovered in two or three months, but forfeited all their pay and prize money.

This was the year that America declared war with England.* All of us who were Americans impressed into the British service, were notoriously insulted and abused by the British officers and men. Often we were brought to the lash so that they could vent their damnable fury on us.

"You damned Yankee," the Captain would say to me, "We'll soon have all your ships in our ports and all your damned countrymen as our prisoners."

I soon had the laugh on him however,† as the first news we had was that my old ship, the *Constitution*, had taken the British *Guerriere*. I wished that the Captain and every Englishman I knew had been on board the *Guerriere* to be blown to hell with her.

* See note 18, page 109.
† See note 19, page 109.

This action between the frigate *Constitution* and their best ship greatly wounded their feelings and gave their pride a check; but it was ill news for us as it increased their ill usage of us. They, to wipe off the slur, said their ship was not half manned.

The truth is that they were out matched by American bravery. Very often the British ships were forced to strike their colors to inferior sail,* as I learned from newspapers and tavern gossip when I went on shore.

After a time, we got information that American seamen impressed into the British service were to give themselves up as prisoners of war and were all to be sent to Dartmoor prison. I thought this good news but was disappointed. There were now about 30 Americans aboard our ship.

We went to the Captain on the quarter deck and asked to deliver ourselves up as prisoners of war. The Captain's name was Nash. I know that there is a hot corner of hell waiting for him.

"Do you call yourself a Yankee,† you damned Scotch rascal?" he shouted to our spokesman. He hit him a hard blow in the face and knocked him down the ladder to the other deck, a distance of about 8 feet.

Upon his recovery, the man came back and of-

* See note 20, page 111.
† See note 21, page 112.

66

fered to show the Captain his protection. The Captain paid no heed to this, promising him that on the first draft of men, he should be sent up the straits or to the East-Indies. The upshot of it all was that many of us were retained, as the Captain said, "to show further proofs of citizenship." The rest were sent away to be massacred in Dartmoor prison.

I was retained because I was a member of Captain Almyer's band of music. This Captain Nash was a violent enemy of all Americans and the only reason why he did not retain us all to butcher us, was because even the British are obliged in some measure to obey the laws of the nations.

In fact, we suffered everything from these treacherous Britons. If we remained upon board ship, the purser cheated us out of the half, if not the whole, of our wages. They were only 32 S per month, and out of this we must furnish all wearing apparel. In fine, all those who went to prison, were the best off. They were not flogged as often.

The Crime of Dartmoor Prison.

THOSE who went to Dartmoor Prison were in another peril. The particulars were related to me by a witness, although I was not there. The prisoners were playing ball in the yard. The ball went over into an adjoining yard where the British arms and ammunition was kept. Some went after the ball.

Immediately a signal was given and these guards fired without mercy upon the unarmed Americans.* I do not know how many were slain by these wretches under arms. It is enough to forever stigmatize the British in the annals of history.

About this time, a memorable action took place between the American privateer *General Armstrong,* commanded by Captain Reed, and the British fleet.† The case was this: the *Armstrong* was lying at Fayal, a neutral port. Finding this out, a British force, greatly superior, arrived. Captain Reed demanded of the governor of the island, permission to come under the fort for protection. He received the reply that the English would not molest him as the port was neutral.

However the American saw fit not to trust the British on any point, neutral or otherwise. So he warped his ship under the fort and came to anchor. He was right; for the following evening he had to beat off a couple of well manned and equipped British boats which came to take him. He beat them off with great slaughter. About 11 o'clock a whole squadron of British boats attacked and one of the sharpest engagements resulted that has ever been recounted in history. The Americans rushed into the British boats and stabbed them at close

* See note 22, page 112.
† See note 23, page 113.

quarters. Our countrymen put the whole stinking, cowardly gang to flight.

On the next morning, the British sent a gun-brig, which anchored alongside, but she received so warm a reception that she was obliged to cut her cables and run for it. About then, a British frigate got under way, to make trial of her force, but the American Captain depressed one of his pieces and fired it through the bottom of his own vessel and made his escape to land, with his crew, in the ship's boats.

The English sent a demand to the governor for the Americans to be delivered over as prisoners. They received the reply that they must come and take the Americans, if they wanted them as prisoners. The British had no taste to do this, after their experience, so they sailed away.

To return to my own affairs. I went on shore for what we sailors call a serious land voyage. Then I returned to my duty, the study of music. I gained some proficiency in both claronet and violin, under a very able Italian master. I now had liberty to go on shore every three weeks and I had 23 months wages due me. I applied to the purser, but he said that, since we were on a guard ship, I could not be paid without an order from our Captain. I wrote to Captain Almyer and laid our necessities before him. So he sent to the office of the admiralty for our abstracts. Then he took us to the navy yard, where we received our pay of 1 P. 12S 6d per month. Out of this, I was required to furnish my own clothing. That had to be of the second best quality, on account of my being a musician. However I could purchase a suit of second hand best superfine for 2 P. 10S. Shirts, handkerchiefs and stockings are also very cheap, but provisions and liquors run high. I have given 18 to 33 S per gallon to carry on board and have then sold it for one-quarter more.

It is very difficult to get spirits on board for it is against the law and as sure as you are detected, you are well flogged. I had a better opportunity than others, as the master of the band was also master of arms. It was his duty to overhaul everyone who came aboard. The business was fully understood between him and me.

So I often smuggled some on the ship and sold it, by which means I had sums of money by me. A sailor has little use for money, however it is well to keep a little on hand, as we fall in with fishing boats and have a chance to purchase fresh fish which is a great luxury after subsisting on salt provisions.

Captain Almyer was now appointed to the command of the frigate *Leonidas*. He brought us on board February 18, 1813. As we stepped on board,

I and two others applied to him and notified him that we wished to deliver ourselves up as prisoners of war and be sent to the prison camp.

He told us he did not consider us as men fighting against our country; but that he would not have forced us to go, if he had had time to write to London about it. However, he said, as we are sailing tomorrow, nothing can be done.

Forced to Fight against Americans.

HE did say that if we came into an action with Americans, he did not wish to ask me to fight. He detained me with these false promises and evasive answers.

We went to Cork as convoy for fourteen merchantmen. Then, after eight days, we sailed on a cruise. Our first capture was the *Dart* of Baltimore, bound for France. She was deep laden with provisions and was the first American ship I saw taken.

She had on board 14 men and in taking her we lost two men; there was a heavy sea when she hove to. She lay so low in the water that, when she rolled, our boats got clinched under her chain plates and broken to pieces. We put a prize master on board and sent her to England. Her crew was taken on board us as prisoners and they received tolerable usage, except their provisions which were extremely bad. As prisoners they had rations to the usual proportion of 4 to six. Their breakfast, for instance, was called "burgoo" and was made by boiling oatmeal in water without anything else, even salt, being added to it.

Then I was drafted on board the *Fortune*, under Captain Grout, until such time as Captain Almyer got his ship which he was to command permanently. This Captain Grout was not so fond of music, so I was ordered to the sail-making business because he heard I had some acquaintance with it and because they had only a few on board that were skilled in that performance. I stayed at this occupation for nearly six months, until we were ordered to Portsmouth and the crew drafted aboard the *Queen*.

When I left to go on the guard ship, the Captain gave me this recommendation:

THESE ARE TO CERTIFY
To every Captain of His Majesty's ships that James R. Durand has served on board His Majesty's ship Fortune, *during which term he behaved with sobriety and attention to his duty and he is in my opinion a very fit man to be a sail-maker.*
Given on board His Majesty's ship Fortune, *this 31st. Day of December 1813.*
William Grout, Capt.

He also wished me to take a warrant and enter the service regularly as a sailmaker, but I refused, as I still had hopes of getting clear. On the ninth day after I went aboard the guard ship, Captain Almyer came to Spithead with his new ship the *Pactolus*. We went on board it January 11, 1814.

So I returned to my practice on musical instruments. I applied again to him for commitment to a prison camp or a discharge, but he answered me that we should sail in the morning for the Downs and that something would be done for me when we got there. We arrived at the Downs, which is 60 or 70 miles from London and the Captain went on shore. He returned in company with the Duke of Cambridge, one of the Royal family. We took the Duke to Holland and put him on shore at a port called Cooks' Haven Bay.

Our men went on shore and purchased long pipes, some made of china and some of silver, which they took to England and sold as curiosities, making double their money.

When we got back to Portsmouth, I thought the Captain would surely do something for me, but here he informed me that, since I had been so long impressed in the service, the admiralty would never consent to discharge me. About this time we heard that Napoleon had made peace.

While waiting off Spithead, I saw a convict ship

ready to sail for Botany Bay in New South Wales, which is a colony three parts around the globe.

We were ordered away. On our journey to Bordeaux, we fell in with the fleet that had the Duchess of Angleane on board, she that is sister to the King of France. As we went into the Bordeaux river, we found it a rendezvous for all the shipping and all of our fleet. General Napoleon was a prisoner, on his way to Elba. I heard he had aged some since I saw him at Goree.*

While we lay there, the aged and wounded troops were sent back to England and the other English soldiers came on board ships to come to America. Some came on board us, too. They said that, since they had whipped Napoleon, they would have no trouble in subduing the U. States. If they had known that Gen. And. Jackson was awaiting them, they would have laughed another way.† We sailed for America in company with 12 transports.

So we sailed June 2nd., 1814 and after a passage of sixty days landed at the Bermudas, in company with the *Pactolus, Tenedos, Pomona* and *Oneida.* The troops were under the command of Admiral Malcolm, as were the ships.

* See note 24, page 118.
† See note 25, page 118.

Off the Shore of New England

WE sailed for New London.

As we drew near my home shores, I asked the Captain what he supposed my countrymen would think, if they knew I was fighting against them.

"In case of attack, you may go below," he replied.

I must here leave it to the reader, to fancy what must be the feelings of a man confined on board a British ship of war for eight or ten years and obliged to undergo every kind of hardship and then, at the last, forced to fight his own father and brother and every kind of kindred. And it was only to satisfy those haughty British tyrants, who are divested of every concern but that of self interest.

We were ordered to attack Stonington. I had some relations living there.

I informed the ship's Captain that I would not fight until the opponents were more to my liking to fight against. I said, "I would rather be hung than fight against the flag of my own country, in the very view of my native shores."

Two other Americans said the same.

Then he ordered the boatswain to make three halters. "I will hang these damned rascals," he said.

The halters were accordingly made and put about our necks. Then he gave us fifteen minutes to change our minds and agree to fight. We would not change our minds.

So then he ordered the master to put us in irons and keep us on maggoty bread and water until we complied with his commands. So we were put in irons.

Commodore Hardy now put the *Vengeance* under way as a bomb ship, together with a despatch brig. They came to anchor direct before the battery at Stonington* and sent a lieutenant on shore with a flag of truce. He demanded the surrender of the town. He told them that if they did not surrender, the civilian inhabitants had only four hours in which to retire, before the British should open fire.

The inhabitants paid no attention to this demand. So the British opened fire and kept it up for a space of 14 hours, without doing any particular damage to the town.

On the other hand, the British received a most destructive fire from the battery, which contained a double fortified 18 pounder and a 12 pounder. These pieces kept up such a continuous fire of well-

* See note 26, page 119.

76

directed shot that our vessels were forced to retire after sustaining much loss and damage.

Some of the American shot went through the brig from stern to stem, dismounting 5 guns, killing 7 men and wounding 17 others. Her spars were so cut that she was about disabled. The *Spencer*, a 74, now got under way to assist the brig, but she grounded on a sand bar and only got off by lightening ship. Her crew were forced to throw overboard her shot racks and other heavy stores. She was afraid of a flotilla of gun boats under command of Commodore Lewis.

Our frigate received a shot from the American artillery which was so well directed that we were obliged to wear out with the tide, to get out of range.

The barges now attempted to land some soldiers at a point beyond the reach of the battery. They were repulsed by the militia, who had the use of a light piece of ordinance. In fact, one barge was taken with 8 or 10 men. The British loss was considerable; a single shot killed a doctor aboard the brig, completely severed the arm from the body of a woman near him and broke several crates of wine bottles.

We were obliged to retreat and it was lucky for the English that we did. The next morning, the Americans received more troops and guns from

New London. They were hoping we would return to the attack, as they had plenty of Yankee trouble waiting for us.

Our Captain stated that this attack cost the British not less than 10,000 P. as every rocket that was thrown cost 5 P.

After repairs, we cruised up and down the sound off Milford and Bridgeport without any capture except one boat. She lowered her sails at the command but the British gave her a volley of musket bullets just the same, breaking a man's leg. The injured man was brought on board. His name was Brainard and he hailed from Brantford. He was given good care and, after his recovery, we sent him on shore.

After this cruise, we sailed to Philadelphia and captured a brig which had once been a British privateer. She was ordered to Halifax. We also took the *Lady Washington*, a sloop bound for Charlestown from New York. Then we returned to our former station at New London.

It was customary with us to send our boats out in the night to capture small craft. We would permit these small craft to ransom themselves at a price that best suited our disposition. When the ransom was so high that they refused it, our officers would burn the craft.

We captured the *Armistice* from New York.

We ordered her to lower her sail, she obeyed; but our commander ordered a full discharge of musketry poured into her quarter, killing some of her crew and wounding others.

We manned her and sent her for Bermuda, but before she reached there she was captured back again by an American privateer and consequently lost to the British prize master and crew.

About this time, news of peace was in circulation. Accordingly we repaired to Bermudas, took despatches and returned to New London, February 25th., 1815. On our arrival there all the ships were dressed in their colors. A grand salute was fired by the ships and complemented by the forts in return. Our officers went on shore by invitation of the American officers, to attend a ball, the most superb that had been exhibited since the Revolution. Both parties were in full military uniform and attended by their guards. They convened at the hotel, with bells ringing and everything illuminated.

I now expected to be put on shore but was disappointed.

So I made the resolve that none of my relatives who had not seen me for 14 years, should meet me as an English sailor. However, I was not able to carry out this plan as a boat came along side with articles for sale. One of the boatmen partly recognized me and inquired my name.

He offered to take a letter to my uncle, who was
in Milford. I wrote to my relative and received an
answer four days later, with an enclosure to my
Captain, demanding my release.

He put me off by saying he had no orders to discharge me in New London. I would not leave without my discharge and my wages which I had labored so hard for.

However, my uncle next wrote to Lyman Law,
Esq., an attorney at New London and also a Member of Congress. Lyman Law came on board to
see me and asked me about the usage, within the
hearing of our Captain. I told him a small part of
what they had done to me and other Americans.

Mr. Law then turned to the Captain and said,
"I want you to give me your word before witnesses
that this man will suffer no more ill-usage from
you or your officers and that he will be discharged
immediately upon your return to Portsmouth."

The Admiral as well as the Captain gave him
their word, although they were quick enough to
break it afterwards. I have heard much about English officers and gentlemen and what their word is
worth, but I never met one whom I would believe
under the most solemn oath. They are and always
will be perjured, lying, sottish, brutal creatures,
arrogant in victory and sullen in defeat. I know

something of them, for as I have indicated, I spent many years in their service.

I might here mention an altercation which took place between Mr. Law and this British officer. Mr. Law positively knew me for an American illegally detained and the other asserted me to be an Englishman, with all the effrontery of which a press gang officer is capable.

We made a quick sail from Montaug Point to Plymouth England, namely sixteen days, although we rode out a gale in the bargain. I now expected my discharge, but the Admiral and the Captain had forgot all the promises they made to Mr. Law. Our ship was sent up for repair and I was as tight in their service as ever. I called the Captain's attention to the promise he had made, but he flogged me for it.

At this time we heard that Napoleon had escaped from Elba and had arrived in France. Our ship was hastily refitted and sent to Bordeaux.

This order made me very uneasy and I earnestly prayed the Captain to secure me my discharge. He only answered that the ship was in a hurry to put to sea; therefore it could not be attended to.

So I wrote to our Consul in London, enclosing a petition for my discharge. Many others who had been impressed were doing likewise. I received a kind letter from the Consul saying he would do all in his power in my behalf. That was all the satisfaction I obtained.

We set sail for France, having two of the French king's generals on board. Our intention was to put into Bordeaux, but we could not.

Next we heard of the battle at Waterloo and that Napoleon had made his escape to Rochford. We now found our way into the Bordeaux River. We lay there some time, during which term Napoleon got into a small island near the mouth of the river with about a thousand troops. He was completely surrounded by the British forces. Then he attempted to escape in a small boat, but seeing the impossibility of managing it, he made for the *Bellerophon*, a 74 gun ship, where he delivered himself up as a prisoner of war. Then the ship sailed for Plymouth with the illustrious prisoner on board. After he had tarried at Plymouth for five or six weeks, he went on board the *Northumberland* to sail for his place of exile, an island called St. Helena.

The presence of this hero excited much curiosity while he was at Plymouth and brought together a great concourse of people. He usually exposed himself to view for two hours a day, to gratify their wishes to see him. He is said to have chosen a retreat or banishment to this solitary island rather than be delivered up to the Russians.

Orders were now given for all the ships to return to England, so that the crews could be paid off and discharged. Our Captain, fearful of losing his authority over us, stayed out as long as he dared, but at length he sailed for Portsmouth. We arrived there September 14th., 1815 and just a week later I received my discharge.

The long wished-for happy hour had arrived, when I again enjoyed my freedom. I received from the Captain the following:

THESE ARE TO CERTIFY
That James R. Durand has served on board His Majesty's ships, the Narcissus *and* Pactolus, *from the 19th. day of October 1809 to September the 21st., 1815; during which time he conducted himself with sobriety and attention, and was always obedient to commands.*
Given under my hand, John Pancher, late Master of the above ships.

After I got my discharge, I proceeded to London to secure my pay in full and, if possible, to obtain a pension for the wounds I received while in the British service. I accordingly took coach and called on the Consul in London, to whom I had formerly sent my protection. I learned there that the former Consul had sent my protection to the British admiralty years before, in an attempt to

83

procure my release from bondage. The admiralty had destroyed it, the Consul supposed.

To protect me against further abuses, I received the following:

AMERICAN CONSULATE AT LONDON

I, Ruben G. Beasley, Consul of the United States of America, for London and the dependencies thereof, do hereby make known and certify to all whom it may concern that JAMES R. DURAND of the town of Milford, State of Connecticut, United States aforesaid, mariner, is a citizen of the United States as appears by proofs produced, to be in force while on his way to the United States.

The said JAMES R. DURAND is twenty-nine years of age, is five feet, three and one half inches high, has a high forehead, hazel eyes, small nose, common mouth; he has a pointed chin, round face, dark hair, dark complexion and is marked with a scar on his right leg.

Given under my hand and official seal in London aforesaid, this twenty-seventh day of September, in the year of our Lord, one thousand, eight hundred and fifteen and of the Independence of the United States, the 40th.

Having called at the Board of the Admiralty and received nothing, not even promises of which the English are usually most liberal, I returned to Plymouth. I found no good employment and my money was growing short.

Then I learned that I was in danger of being impressed a second time, as the press gangs were working busily. Therefore I hastened back to London dock and found a ship clearing for New York. I asked the Captain if he would give me a passage to the U. States, but he refused, unless I came with an order from the Consul. I procured the order and delivered it to Captain Day of New London, who commanded the ship *Nabby* of that port.

I now set sail, losing my effects in Plymouth, to the value of 20 P. or more, as I dared not go back there for them lest I be marked by a press gang. I paid my last respects to London on January 18th., 1816 and arrived in New York on the 19th. day of March following.

For the information of the reader I will here set down a slight description of London as it fell under my observation.

It was founded between the reign of Julius Caesar and Nero's time, as is supposed, although this is a matter of uncertainty. It is, however, historically sure that it was walled by the great Emperor Constantine.

Its length, at this age, is nearly eight miles; its breadth, three, and its circumference is twenty-six. It is situated on the River Thames, which is continually filled with fleets from all parts of the globe.

But I will refer other details to abler historians.

The only accident of our passage from London to New York was that the ship took fire. Some bottles of Aqua Fortis were broken. Before the flames could be extinguished several of the passengers were badly burned. However, we put a stop to the danger by throwing the Aqua Fortis overboard.

I landed at Milford from the New Haven packet. I received a hearty welcome from all my friends and relations whom I found in good health.

It is my wish that the foregoing pages will be a sufficient admonition to all youths to avoid the snares and usages of the English men-of-wars-men.

Yours Most Resp.

JAMES R. DURAND.

Rochester, N.Y., 1820.

Notes.

1. "Bound apprentices to a farmer."

By 1792, some beginnings at government had been made. Washington, much against his own wish, was running for reëlection. Coinage of United States currency had begun. Kentucky had been added to the Union and General Wayne was building up an army to drive the raiding Indians from Ohio.

The country warmed with enthusiasm over the news of a revolution in France. If Durand had been bound as an apprentice in Boston, he might have seen the magnificent civic celebration.

"An Ox, roasted Whole was placed on a Waggon drawn by Sixteen Horses, while on the horns of the Ox were displayed the Flags of the American and French Republics. Carts followed, bearing bread and two Hogsheads of Strong Punch, which was distributed Free to the Populace."

Of American society, as it then existed, a visitor wrote:

> Take Christians, Mohawks, Democrats and all
> From the rude wigwam to the Congress Hall.
> From man, the savage, whether tamed or free,
> To man, the civilized, less tamed than he;
> 'Tis one dull chaos, one infertile strife
> Betwixt half-polished and half-barbarous life;
> Whatever ill the ancient world can brew
> Is mixed with every grossness of the new;
> Where all corrupts, though little can entice,
> And nothing's known of luxury but vice.

87

AN ABLE SEAMAN OF 1812

2. "With him I . . . found a home and a friend."

The uncle was a selectman. Of these worthies Adams said, "The towns were managed by selectmen, the elected instruments of town meetings, whose jealousy of granting power was even greater than their objection to spending money; and whose hostility to city government was not to be overcome" (Henry Adams, *History of the United States 1801-1816*).

3. "I again resolved to try the seas."

Durand's decision to become a sailor does not imply any love for the sea or ships. In 1801 a sailor's life could have been termed the least of many evils.

With Jefferson's election came a time of acute business depression. In 1801 money was cautious and there was little or nothing in the expansion of the commercial world to tempt a boy of Durand's type.

Life in the army was not attractive. The men were underpaid, underfed and overworked. On the sea, however, there was a constant demand for able-bodied sailors.

In 1800 the total population of the United States was 5,300,000, somewhat less than the present population of New York City proper. These inhabitants were scattered along the Atlantic coast, two thirds of them living within fifty miles of tidewater.

New England, in those days, was no paradise. In 1808 Wilson, the ornithologist, said of his trip: "My journey rather lowered the Yankees in my esteem. Except for a few neat academies, I found their school houses equally ruinous and deserted with ours; their fields were covered with stones; their orchards wretched; they have scarcely

one grain field in twenty miles; the taverns along the
road are dirty and filled with loungers brawling about
law suits and politics; the people are snappish, extor-
tioners and lazy."

President Dwight of Yale mentioned the turnpike road
across Rhode Island, which was constructed about this
time. The citizens of Providence expended upon their
part of the highway the whole sum of money appropriated by the legislature. The turnpike corporation then
applied to the legislature for enough additional money
to complete the work.

The lawmakers refused this reasonable petition. One
of the members explained his refusal by saying that
taxation for an established church and turnpikes was an
English custom. England was a monarchy. Citizens of
Massachusetts and Connecticut were obliged by law to
support ministers. Therefore the citizens of Massachusetts and Connecticut were slaves, even as the English.

"But, thank God," continued President Dwight's sar-
castic paraphrase of the old patriots' logic, "free-born
Rhode Islanders will never submit to be priest-ridden nor
to be forced to pay for the privilege of traveling in the
mud."

So it happened that the road was not completed for
several years.

It was about that time the earliest temperance movement began "because of the practice of some ministers
who ascended their pulpits to preach, when drunk"
(Adams).

President Dwight said his people were "contented
with college commencements and sleigh riding" for
recreation. He thought the theater immoral and considered whist "an unhappy dissipation."

It is not remarkable that lively youths like Durand moved away from New England villages as soon as possible.

Those who went west found little that was attractive or profitable. Life in a Kentucky cabin meant "eat salt pork three times a day, seldom or never have any vegetables and drink ardent spirits from morning to night" (Ashe, 1806).

So great was the prejudice against frontier life that the optimistic Jefferson said it would require "a thousand years" to settle the wilderness.

These are some of the estimates of conditions made by shrewd contemporary writers. It is no cause for surprise that Durand, like other boys of his day and race, chose life on the sea as less monotonous, more pleasing, more adventurous, and more promising of reward.

4. "I agreed for that sum" [eight dollars a month].

Because of the scarcity of coined money, this may be considered a very fair wage. Some idea of the purchasing power of money at that time may be obtained from President Dwight's eulogy of Abijah Weld, pastor of Attleborough.

According to the head of Yale College, Weld maintained a hospitable home, gave charity to the poor, and brought up eleven children upon his salary of $240 a year.

5. "An English man-of-war boat alongside to overhaul the ship's crew."

Great Britain and the United States were "getting on each other's nerves." In another place (page 131) some of the English complaints will be enumerated. It seems fair to state that the Americans were like the English in their aggressions, although not so frequently at fault, because the British showed a more formidable front.

Perhaps the truth is simply that England could not remember the United States had grown up and was now "too big to spank;" while the United States could not forget the spankings England had attempted to administer.

There was constant trouble on the Canadian border. On the sea, the British insisted upon the right of search of American vessels, under the excuse of looking for deserters from the King's navy. On the other hand, well-informed British authorities claimed, with much parade of fact, that Americans took great delight in inducing English sailors to desert.

Other and more important excuses for war were present in abundance. But these might have been adjusted. It is usually a minor difficulty which makes peace impossible.

Furthermore, there was trouble with France.

France resented the fact that the United States had not joined her in declaring war on England, Holland, and Spain simultaneously. French raids upon American commerce were followed by the American envoy's declaration that a bribe had been demanded as the price of peace between the two countries. To this demand Pinckney made his famous retort, "Millions for defense, but not one cent for tribute."

A half-war actually followed (1797-1800). It was made the excuse for much raiding of merchant shipping by privateers. One or two first-rate naval battles were fought. Then a peace was made with Napoleon, who had become First Consul.

From newspaper editorials of that time it would appear that both countries were ready to fight, but were prevented by difficulties of transportation. In reality, the whole thing was a flurry which did not entirely end with the treaty of peace. It might be termed a part of the growing pains of both countries.

A third international difficulty was between the Barbary States on the northern coast of Africa and the United States. This was a simple matter. The Barbary rulers were pirates, engaged in the hold-up business. The United States, being a new nation, was a new victim.

6. "I beheld the most horrid sight which my eyes were ever to witness."

Durand, looking at the Slaves' Rebellion through a porthole, saw some of the butcheries, which was about as much as any observer saw.

A mixed company of French and English planters held Haiti until 1697, when the entire island was ceded to France: The slave population was tremendous. Plantations, worked by this slave labor, prospered until 1789, when the French Revolution broke out.

The ideal of "liberty" has a strange habit of not knowing where to stop. The blacks and mulattoes appealed to it and, in 1791, the French Convention—"For a Frenchman would rather die than be illogical" (Fiske)—declared the slaves to be free. So, in spite of the protests of the planters, a sort of universal suffrage was granted.

The freed men ran wild. The convention's order unleashed a power which threatened to sweep every white, and later, every mulatto, off the island. To save themselves and their property, the planters turned traitors and invited the English to send an army to seize the island and restore order.

One man stands out as a heroic figure, far above all his contemporaries, during the years of chaos and violence that followed. He was Toussaint L'Ouverture, black descendant of African kings—"The best, bravest and most brilliant man his race has ever produced" (Fiske). He first warred against the French planters until the rights of the slaves had been established in the Paris Convention.

Then L'Ouverture, in return for French citizenship, led his black army against the English expeditionary force which had landed. As a general, the negro showed that he has had few equals or superiors in modern history. After six years of desperate fighting, Toussaint drove the English from the island.

But Napoleon was now consul and he did not share the convention's sympathy for slaves. When the French minister called Napoleon's attention to the fact that L'Ouverture had framed a constitution and had been elected the first president of Haiti, Napoleon revoked the decree of liberty for the blacks and sent a veteran army to subdue them.

Some 25,000 French troops failed to conquer in the field. Then Toussaint was captured by treachery, under a flag of truce, and sent to France to rot and die in a dungeon. It has been called the "vilest act of Napoleon's career." After this despicable victory, the French were driven off by a British fleet.

Durand might have viewed the sights he enumerates at almost any time between 1789 and 1803.

L'Ouverture had a successor if not an equal. Dessalines made himself governor for life. He celebrated his inauguration with a massacre of every white he could find and in 1804 proclaimed himself emperor of Haiti. Two years later he was assassinated by his subjects.

Since that day the unhappy island has been torn by every manner of revolt, factional war, bloody dictatorship, and revolution. "On the whole, it must be owned that, after a century of independence and self-government, the Haitian people have made no progress, if, indeed, they have not shown signs of retrogression" (*Encyclopædia Britannica*).

7. "We gave one privateer a broadside that dismasted her."

There was then no formal war with France. It had ended in September of 1800. But according to the free and easy naval customs of the time, privateers were known to act upon the supposition that another war might have started since they quitted their home port.

Many, perhaps most, privateers were little more than legalized pirates. The custom of fitting out privateers died out among nations because "the risk of capture became greater than the chance of profits" (Adams).

8. [From] "Wilmington in North Carolina and then traveled to Baltimore."

This was no Pullman car jaunt. Wilson, a contemporary traveler, said:

"The taverns [of North Carolina] are the most desolate and beggarly imaginable; bare, bleak and dirty walls, while two or three old broken chairs and a bench form all the furniture. At supper you sit down to a meal the very sight of which is sufficient to deaden the most eager appetite. You are surrounded by half-a-dozen, half-naked blacks, male and female, whom any man of common scent might nose a quarter of a mile off. The white females seldom make their appearance.

"The house is raised upon props four or five feet and the space below is left open for the hogs. With their charming vocal performances the wearied traveler is serenaded the whole night long."

9. "Entered the United States service for . . . war against the Turks."

In 1790 President Washington called the attention of Congress to the depredations made upon American vessels by the Mediterranean pirates. Secretary of State Jefferson, in his annual report of that year, included several details of this "tariffa" which the robber beys levied.

The first American commissioner sent to treat with the Bey of Algiers asked that potentate to agree to stop his raids upon our shipping. He received this remarkable reply:

"If I make peace with you, I should make peace with everybody. And if I make peace with everybody, what should I do with my corsairs? What should I do with my soldiers? They would take off my head for want of other prizes, as they would not be able to live on what I could pay them" (Lossing).

So, in the spring of 1794, Congress appropriated

nearly $700,000 to provide a naval armament, with the intention of wiping out this menace to shipping. But the ships could not be built over-night. The need was immediate, so the next year a contract was signed with the Bey of Algiers. At that time the Bey was holding 15 captured American ships and 180 enslaved American seamen. The United States paid $800,000 as ransom for the captives, delivered to the Bey a frigate valued at $100,-000 and agreed to pay an annual tribute of $23,000 (Lossing). This sum was paid annually from 1795 until 1812.

With the signing of this humiliating contract, the work was stopped on the keels of the three frigates which had been laid down. Two years later, when war impended with France, President Adams put pressure upon Congress to appropriate the money to complete and fit the ships. As a result, the frigates *United States, Constitution,* and *Constellation* were launched (Lossing).

In the meantime, Congress created a Navy Department, and April 30, 1798, Benjamin Stoddard of Georgetown was appointed Secretary of the Navy.

Not long after her launching, the frigate *Constellation* received her baptism of fire. In February of 1799 she captured the French frigate *L'Insurgente,* which had previously captured the American schooner *Retaliation.* The next year the *Constellation* was badly battered in an action with the French *La Vengeance.* In this engagement, the American casualties were 161 killed and wounded. These were the chief battles of the Franco-American war (Lossing).

Seamen were being trained to the work of a man-of-war and it was due to this French scare that the United

States came to possess a navy which could cope with the pirates and, later, with the British.

At that time, the phrase "Algerian pirates" was used loosely to indicate any members of the Barbary States: Morocco, Algiers, Tunis, and Tripoli. These Turkish dependencies were then in the heyday of their prosperity.

Captain Bainbridge, commanding the frigate *George Washington,* arrived at Algiers in September of 1800, to pay the annual tribute money to the Bey. That ruler, in the casual tone one would use in ordering up a taxi, commanded Bainbridge to take an ambassador from the Bey's court to Constantinople.

Bainbridge objected that the United States frigate was no common carrier.

"You pay me tribute," replied the Bey. "By that act you become my slaves. Therefore I order you as I see proper."

The *George Washington* was anchored under the loaded cannons of the castle and batteries. A refusal meant that his frigate would be destroyed. Bainbridge did as the Bey ordered and delivered the ambassador at Constantinople. His was the first vessel to fly the American flag off the Sultan's capital. The Sultan said that he regarded the stars upon it as a favorable omen for friendship between the two countries. "For," he explained, "the stars belong in the same sky with my crescent" (Lossing).

Jefferson was now president. His administration favored neither the construction nor maintenance of warships as heavy as frigates. (See Tom Paine's *Plan for National Defense by Gun Boats.*) Such mammoth ships of the line, in Republican minds, were merely an invitation to this country to pick a fight with other nations (Adams).

But the Bey's insult and other incidents convinced the President and cabinet members that, since they already had the frigates, the navy might as well practice on the pirates with them.

Commodore Morris was sent with a force to blockade the pirates' ports. He was so inactive he was called home and dismissed (Adams). His successor, Commodore Preble, reached Gibraltar in 1803, expecting to have in his fleet the frigates *Constitution,* 44 guns; *Philadelphia,* 38 guns; the brigs *Argus* and *Siren,* 16 guns; *Nautilus* and *Vixen,* 14 guns; and the *Enterprise,* 12 guns.

However, on Preble's arrival, he was greeted with the news that the *Philadelphia,* her officers and crew, were in the hands of the pirates. She had been lost through overzeal.

Bainbridge, still smarting after his treatment by the Bey, was in command of the *Philadelphia.* While chasing a native boat, the frigate grounded on a rock and before Bainbridge's crew could float her off, she was surrounded by an overwhelming number of gunboats. Bainbridge was abundantly justified in striking his colors. The officers were treated as prisoners of war, but the members of the crew were enslaved at hard labor.

The Yankee seamen in Preble's fleet despised their opponents and it galled them to see the pirates take one trick in the game. Their first reply to the Bey of Tripoli was a daring bit of Yankee ingenuity.

The Bey of Tripoli sent a present to the Sultan. It was sent on a small sailing vessel. The present was a singing and dancing chorus of slave girls for the Sultan's permanent light opera company and harem. The Americans captured the vessel, present and all. History does not record what became of the harem beauties, but the boat was rechristened the *Intrepid* and placed under the command of Lieutenant Stephen Decatur (Lossing).

Decatur, with 73 men, sailed the converted vessel past the harbor batteries into the port of Tripoli. Without being detected, Decatur and his men anchored alongside the captive *Philadelphia,* which was moored below heavy shore batteries. Then, boarding the *Philadelphia,* they killed or drove overboard the Turkish prize crew, set the frigate on fire, watched her until it was certain she would be consumed, ran out of the harbor past the thundering batteries and escaped, without the loss of a man.

The Bey, enraged at the capture of the girls and the burning of the prize, threw the prisoners from the *Philadelphia* into the "most degrading form of servitude" (Lossing).

10. "Midshipmen who are mere boys."

"And as a ship's complement always consists of a great proportion of boys, and very young ones, too, while scarcely any boys are to be seen on an American ship, it would be considering men and boys as equal in effectiveness not to list them separately" (British source —James, *Naval History*).

From a Charlestown editor's letter: "The crew of the *Dominica,* with the exception of eight or ten boys, were fine looking young men. . . . Among the members of her crew is a small boy, not eleven years old, who was twice wounded while contending for victory on her deck."

The use of boys seems to have been so universal that few writers commented upon it.

11. "The United States frigate *President* . . . informed
   us of a treaty" [with Tripoli].

Durand is sadly mistaken in the dates he has indicated.
It seems likely that his various voyages and the events
which he saw on each had become confused in his mind.

12. "The *Constitution* was commanded by Commodore
   Rodgers."

Commodore John Rodgers was the first of several
celebrated naval officers of his family. He entered the
government service in 1797 and as a junior officer on the
Constellation helped to capture the French *L'Insurgente*.

"He was advanced until he became commander of the
Mediterranean squadron and, as such, brought Tripoli
and Tunis to final terms. He also presided at the court
martial of Commodore Barron for the loss of the *Chesapeake*. Because of this, Commodore Rodgers narrowly
escaped a duel with Commodore Barron's brother who
later killed Stephen Decatur" (A. H. Ulm).

The first John Rodgers's oldest son became the first
rear admiral of the navy. The fourth naval officer of the
name in 1925 commanded the PN-9 on the Hawaii flight.

13. "Their cannon made a tremendous thunder."

This was the battle of Trafalgar (October 21, 1805),
"which was a sequel to the breakdown of Napoleon's
great scheme for the invasion of England" (*Encyclopædia Britannica*).

The British fleet under Nelson defeated and destroyed
the combined French and Spanish fleets. Nelson was
killed. Napoleon's navy was gone forever.

NOTES

14. "We said that the man should not be punished."

Adams mentions the mutiny on the *Constitution*. However, Durand's account of it is more detailed than others which are quoted in the official documents. His story seems to be a fair and accurate description of the affair.

15. "We heard of the action between the . . . *Chesapeake* and the . . . *Leopard*."

According to Durand's date, he heard of this incident some six months before it happened.

On May 16, 1806, Great Britain declared a blockade of the whole coast from the Elbe in Germany to Brest in France. Napoleon promptly countered by declaring a paper blockade of all ports in the British Isles. American vessels attempting to run either were seized almost indiscriminately by both sides.

The English also continued to search American vessels for alleged deserters from the British navy, a practice which began almost as soon as the Revolution ended. In 1796 and 1797, for instance, the American minister in London made application for the release of 271 seamen who had been illegally seized by press gangs. The British authorities paid as little attention to these complaints as the warring nations, during the World War, heeded the protests of neutrals.

The only prosperous industry of any magnitude in the United States at that time was the shipping and export trade. Hot-headed merchants and shipowners clamored for war.

In the early summer of 1807 a British fleet was lying off Chesapeake Bay. The British officers claimed four seamen, members of the crew of the frigate *Chesapeake,* as deserters from the British frigate *Melampus.* Commodore Barron refused to give up the men.

On June 22 the *Chesapeake* quitted the Virginia Capes on her way to the Mediterranean, where she was supposed to relieve the *Constitution.* She was overtaken by the British frigate *Leopard* almost within sight of land.

The commander of the *Leopard* carried this written order from his superior, Admiral Berkeley. Berkeley had issued it without authority from his government.

"Where-as many seamen, subjects of His Britannic Majesty and serving in his ships and vessels . . . while at anchor in the Chesapeake, deserted and entered on board the United States' frigate called *Chesapeake* and openly paraded in the streets of Norfolk, in the sight of their officers . . . under the American flag, protected by the magistrates of the town and the recruiting officer belonging to the above-mentioned American frigate, which magistrates and recruiting officer refused giving them up. . . .

"The Captains and Commanders of His Majesty's ships and vessels under my command are hereby required and directed, in case of meeting the *Chesapeake* at sea and without the limits of the United States, to show the Captain this order and to require to search his ship for deserters . . . and to proceed and search for the same. And if a similar demand be made by the American . . . he is to be permitted to search for any deserters . . . according to the customs and usages of civilized nations. . . ."

This order did not say it required the use of force. But any British captain reading it must have given thought to what he would do if the *Chesapeake* refused, as it was obvious she would. The British captain could only answer his own question by saying "use force."

"The inefficiency of our government . . . was shown even more strikingly in the story of the *Chesapeake* than in the conspiracy of Burr. The frigate *Constitution* had sailed for the Mediterranean in August, 1803. The government knew that her crew were entitled to discharge and the President had no right to withhold it. No emergency existed. A single ship (to relieve the *Constitution*) needed to be fitted out for the sea at a date fixed three years beforehand. Yet, when the time came and the *Constitution* ought to have reached home, the *Chesapeake* had not so much as begun preparation. Captain James Barron was selected to command her as Commodore of the Mediterranean squadron" (Adams).

"Such was the inefficiency of the navy yard. . . . Captain Gordon tried to fire a salute from the *Chesapeake* (while passing Mt. Vernon) and discovered neither the sponges nor cartridges would go in the guns" (Adams).

After numerous delays, on the morning of June 22, the *Chesapeake* sailed. She paid no attention to the fact that the British *Leopard, Bellonia,* and *Melampus* were watching every move. As the *Chesapeake* drew away from land, she was followed by the *Leopard*. Some distance out, the *Leopard* signaled to say she had despatches for the American. This betrayed no hostile purpose.

"Doubtless Barron ought not to have allowed a foreign ship of war to come alongside without calling his crew to quarters; but the condition of the ship made it inconvenient to clear the guns and the idea of an attack was so extravagant that, as Barron said afterwards, he might as well have expected one while at anchor in Hampton Roads" (Adams).

A young British lieutenant came on board with a note which contained the British admiral's order. It concluded with the polite hope that nothing would follow to disturb the harmony between the two countries. Barron immediately sent back a polite refusal of the request for a search. He added that his own orders forbade him to permit his crew to be mustered by any but his own officers.

"Such an answer to such a demand was little suited . . . to check a British officer. . . . If Barron had wished to invite an attack, he could have done nothing more to the purpose than by receiving Berkeley's orders without a movement for self-defense" (Adams).

About five minutes after the British lieutenant left, the American commander ordered his officers to clear for action without drumbeat or display. To clear the ship required at least a half-hour. Immediately came a hail from the *Leopard* and a shot across the *Chesapeake's* bow. Another followed, and then three full broadsides were fired at two or three hundred feet, pointblank into the American hull. The *Chesapeake* was helpless and after seeing his crew slaughtered for fifteen minutes, Commodore Barron struck his colors.

Only one gun was fired by the *Chesapeake* in reply to the solid shot and canister of the *Leopard*. This single gun was fired by Third Lieutenant Allen. According to the custom of the service, the guns on the *Chesapeake* were charged with powder and shot. They were discharged by touching off with logger-heads kept in the magazine and heated in the galley stove whenever need

arose. Of course the logger-heads were not hot and Lieutenant Allen carried a live coal in his fingers from the
stove to the gun, in order to discharge it.

As soon as the *Chesapeake's* colors were down, the
British came aboard, searched the ship with many apolo-
gies more galling than their solid shot, selected three
American-born sailors who had deserted the *Melampus*
after being impressed upon her and dragged Seaman
Jenkin Ratford out of the coal hole where he was hiding.
Ratford was English-born and a deserter.

Three members of the *Chesapeake's* crew were killed
and about twenty wounded.

"Disgraced and degraded, with officers and crew
smarting under a humiliation that was never forgotten
or forgiven, the unlucky *Chesapeake* dragged her way
back to Norfolk. . . . Public sentiment required a victim.
Barron was brought before a court martial, January 4,
1808" (Adams).

Barron was held blameless on every count save one.
He was not negligent of his duty; not to blame for not
having called his crew to quarters when first signaled;
but he was held wrong in failing to prepare for action
the minute he read Admiral Berkeley's order. Barron
was suspended from the service for five years without
pay or emoluments.

"Barron's punishment was not likely to stimulate caution in the naval service. For no American captain, unless he wished to be hung by his own crew from his own
yard arm, was ever likely to allow a British frigate to
come within gunshot, without taking such precautions
as he would have taken against a pirate" (Adams).

Admiral Berkeley wrote his approval of the affair to

Captain Humphreys of the *Leopard* (dated July 4th):
"You have conducted yourself most properly. . . . I
hope you mind the published accounts . . . as little as
I do. . . . We must make allowances for the state of the
populace in a country where law and every tie, both civil
and religious, is treated so lightly" (Marshall's *Naval
Biography*).

This attitude of a naval commander whose captain, by
his order, had just committed an act so lawless that his
government was forced to disown it, explains much of
Britain's conduct. The admiral hanged Jenkin Ratford
and ordered the three American sailors to receive five
hundred lashes. The flogging was never given, the sailors
remaining in prison.

A wave of indignation followed the spreading of the
news of this incident through the States. A loud cry for
war with England was heard "from pulpit and grog shop,
from college and counting house alike." The navy was
only too eager to avenge it and did so before war was
declared. Yankee seamen had a habit of paying obligations of this kind, with a very careful reckoning of the
interest due their opponents.

In 1811 Captain John Rodgers sailed the frigate *President* from Annapolis, with orders to protect American
merchant ships from British cruisers, which were active
in impressing sailors. His orders included instructions
to "vindicate the injured honor of the navy and revive
the drooping spirits of the Nation . . . to maintain and
support at any cost the honor of the Flag" as Secretary
Hamilton carefully mentioned, "because of the inhuman
and dastardly attack on our frigate *Chesapeake*."

Within a few miles of the scene of the *Chesapeake-*

Leopard engagement, on the evening of May 16, 1811, Rodgers overtook an English sail which he supposed to be the *Guerrière*. His story was that, as soon as he hailed her, he received a shot for a reply.

Officers and crew were burning for a fight. They were at their quarters and had the ship cleared almost before the order was given. Nor was there any difficulty about cold logger-heads. The *Guerrière* had been particularly hated for acts of oppression. As soon as the enemy gun was fired, or perhaps before, the Americans began to serve their own guns for twenty-five minutes of intensive artillery practice and almost blew their opponent out of the water. When she struck, she proved to be not the *Guerrière* but the *Little Belt*.

Rodgers was genuinely grieved to learn she was much lighter than his own vessel and not an equal opponent, as the *Guerrière* would have been. The *Little Belt* lost eleven killed and twenty-one wounded, principal and interest on the *Chesapeake* debt. Rodgers's loss was one boy wounded.

Both nations conducted inquiries into the affair. Commanders and crews of both vessels fully cleared themselves of any wrongdoing or aggressive action, to the satisfaction of their own governments. But each story was a direct contradiction of the other.

A few weeks later an English envoy arrived in Washington, prepared to give full reparation for the *Chesapeake* incident. He found that no one took time to listen to him. He was informed, unofficially, that "Rodgers had taken up the claim" and instead of giving an indemnity, the envoy was forced to ask for one.

AN ABLE SEAMAN OF 1812

16. "Our Captain, considering my forwardness in taking
and securing these boats, gave me better usage."

British navy officers seemed to hold a high opinion of
Americans as fighting men. Frequent comments are made,
although sometimes in a sneering tone, of the capabilities
of the Yankees as fighters and navigators. But Michael
Scott ("Tom Cringle's Log"—*Blackwood's Magazine,*
1829-1830) gave an estimate which is worth repeating.

Scott, born in Glasgow in 1789, lived in Jamaica, the
West Indies, for many years. He was a careful observer
and shrewd commentator upon men and events between
1806 and 1817. "More of contemporary life can be
learned from Scott than from all the official papers and
documents of the time" (Adams).

"I don't like Americans," Scott said. "I never did and
I never shall. I have seldom met an American gentleman,
in the large and complete sense of the term. I have no
wish to eat with them, drink with them, deal or consort
with them in any way. But let me tell the whole truth—
nor to fight with them, were it not for the laurels to be
acquired by overcoming an enemy so brave, determined,
alert and in every way so worthy of one's steel as they
have always proved.

"In the field, or grappling in mortal combat on the
blood-slippery quarter deck of an enemy's vessel, a British soldier or sailor is the bravest of the brave. No soldier
or sailor of any country, *saving and excepting always
those damned Yankees,* can stand against them."

(*The italics and punctuation do not appear in the
original.*)

17. "My reputation for courage in a fight prevented my being discharged."

Durand was not the only American prisoner who was found "too good to be discharged."

"The British were keen to impress American sailors, who proved themselves the best seamen in the King's navy. For that reason the British were loath to abandon their practice of search and seizure" (Lossing).

18. "This was the year that America declared war with England."

War was declared June 18, 1812. "Insult after insult was offered to the American flag. The British press insolently boasted 'The United States can not be kicked into a war.' Forbearance was no longer a virtue" (Lossing).

19. "I soon had the laugh on him however, as the first news we had was that my old ship, the *Constitution*, had taken the British *Guerriere*."

"By one of the most remarkable feats of seamanship ever recorded" (Adams) the *Constitution* escaped capture at the hands of the entire British fleet. This was only a short time after war was declared, when the frigate stumbled into an enemy cruising squadron. The chase lasted for days before the *Constitution* showed the last pair of sail her heels.

Commodore Hull, then commanding the *Constitution*, had the good fortune to run across the British *Guerrière*,

AN ABLE SEAMAN OF 1812

August 19, 1812, when the *Guerrière* was separated from
the rest of the fleet. The hatred was intense on both sides.
Every American wished to see the English ship humbled,
for she had been most offensive. The English, on the
other hand, were burning with a hope of revenge for the
Little Belt incident. Thus a naval battle became a sort
of personal duel.

For nearly an hour the ships jockeyed for position.
Then, since everyone on both sides was eager for action,
they closed on equal terms, "coming together, side by
side, within pistol shot." The wind was almost astern
and they ran before it, pounding each other with mighty
broadsides (Adams).

In thirty minutes (Hull's report) the *Guerrière* was
"left without a spar standing and her hull was cut to
pieces in such a manner as to make it difficult for her to
keep above water."

"That Dacres [commanding the *Guerrière*] should
have been defeated was not surprising; that he should
have expected to win was an example of British arro-
gance that explained and excused the war. . . . In every
respect, in proportion of ten to seven, the *Constitution*
was the better ship. Her crew was more numerous in
proportion of ten to six. Dacres knew this nearly as well
as Hull. What he did not know was that, in a still greater
proportion, the American officers and crew were better
and more intelligent seamen than the British and that
their passion to repay old scores gave them extraordinary
energy" (Adams).

"However small the affair might appear on the general
scale of the world's battles, it raised the United States

in one short half-hour to the rank of a first class power in the world. Hull's famous victory taught the pleasures of war to a new generation. . . . The first taste of blood maddens. Hardly had the *Constitution* reached port and told her story than the public became eager for more" (Adams).

20. "Very often the British ships were forced to strike their colors to inferior sail."

"During the six months that the war had [then] lasted, the little United States navy captured three British frigates, besides the 20-gun *Alert* and the 18-gun *Frolic*. Privateers by scores had ravaged British commerce, while the immense British force on the ocean had succeeded in capturing the little *Nautilus*, the 12-gun brig *Vixen* and the *Wasp*. The commerce of America had, indeed, suffered almost total destruction; but the dispute was to be decided not so much by the loss which England could inflict upon America as by that which America could inflict upon England" (Adams).

At that time "the British navy consisted of almost 900 vessels with crews of 144,000 men. The American vessels of war of large size, numbered only 12, mounting about 300 guns. . . . The Americans were greatly elated by these victories. National privateers now swarmed upon the ocean, making prizes. Accounts of their exploits filled the newspapers. It is estimated that, during the year 1812, some 50 British armed vessels, 250 merchantmen, 3,000 prisoners and a vast amount of booty were captured by the Americans" (Lossing).

21. " 'Do you call yourself a Yankee, you damned Scotch rascal?' "

Treating an impressed American as a Scotchman was evidently a favorite ruse of British sea captains. See *The Adventures of M'Lean,* page 125.

22. "These guards fired without mercy upon the unarmed Americans."

Again Durand is mistaken about his dates. The Dartmoor massacre was April 6, 1815, several months after peace had been declared. No butchery of which we have a record was less necessary. In a curious old publication, *A Journal of a Young Man of Massachusetts,* are gathered many affidavits of prisoners and witnesses of the massacre. The stories bear out Durand's version, except, of course, they contain a great amount of detail.

The British admiralty so "whitewashed" the commandant of the prison for his responsibility in the shooting, that the British government never made any attempt at punishment or compensation. As a post-war crime, it seems to match the affair of an American frigate that fired into a British East Indian boat, although the British officers bellowed out that the war was over.

Perhaps in the Dartmoor case one of the affidavits of the prisoners sheds some light on the cause.

"Some of the British soldiers observed when receiving one of the wounded men, 'This is in turn for New Orleans,' (Jackson's victory) 'where you killed our men. Now we have our revenge.' "

Only a few days before the massacre the commandant was prevented by one of his subordinates from ordering a wholesale execution. The Americans claimed, with much

NOTES
===

reason, that they had no cause to attempt to escape, since
they were to be released within a few weeks or even days.

23. "A memorable action . . . between the American
privateer *General Armstrong* . . . and the British
fleet."

History agrees with Durand's version of the battle.
It is a real temptation to print in full the letter which
the American commander of the privateer sent home to
his owners.

"Fayal 4th. Oct. 1814

"With infinite regret I am constrained to say it has
eventually fallen to my lot to state to you the loss and
total destruction of the private armed brig, *General Armstrong,* late under my command. . . . [Here follows a
description of his orders and maneuvers during the engagement and a bluff, seaman's story of the fight.] . . .
By what I have been able to learn from the British consul and officers of the fleet, there were about 400 men
and officers in the last attack by the boats, of which 120
were killed and 130 wounded. Captain Lloyd (British
commander) is badly wounded in the leg. . . . It is said,
however (by the British) that the wound was occasioned
by an ox treading on him. . . .

"The loss on my part, I am happy to say, is comparatively trifling—two killed and seven wounded. With re-
gard to my officers in general, I feel the greatest satisfaction in saying, they, one and all, fought with the most
determined bravery and to them I feel highly indebted
for their officer-like conduct. . . . Their exertions and
bravery deserved a better fate. . . .

"I remain, Gentlemen, your very obedient and hum-
ble servant,
"Samuel C. Reid."

AN ABLE SEAMAN OF 1812

A much greater tribute to the American sailors, and to their commander, is paid in this letter of an English witness.

"Fayal, October 15, 1814.

"William Cobbett, Esq.,

"Sir:

"The American schooner privateer *General Armstrong* of New York, Captain Samuel G. Reid, of 7 guns and 90 men entered here on the 26th. ult., about noon, 17 days from New York, for the purpose of taking water. The captain, seeing nothing upon the horizon, was induced to anchor. Before the elapse of many hours, His Majesty's brig *Carnation* came in and anchored near her. About six, His Majesty's ship *Plantagenet* of 74 guns and the *Rota,* frigate, came in and anchored also.

"The captain of the privateer and his friends consulted the first authorities here about her security. They all considered the privateer perfectly secure and that His Majesty's officers were too well acquainted with the respect due to a neutral port to molest her. But to the great suprise of everyone, about nine o'clock in the evening, four boats were dispatched, armed and manned from His Majesty's ships, for the purpose of cutting her out.

"It being about full of the moon, the night perfectly calm and clear, we could see every movement made. The boats approached rapidly toward her, when it appears, the captain of the privateer hailed them and told them to keep off, several times. They, notwithstanding, pushed on and were in the act of boarding before any defense was made on the privateer.

"A warm contest ensued on both sides. The boats

114

were finally dispersed with great loss. The American, now calculating on a very superior force being sent, cut his cables and rowed the privateer close in, alongside the fort. The Governor now sent a remonstrance to Van Lloyd (Captain) of the *Plantagenet,* against such proceedings. And he trusted that the privateer would not be further molested, she being in the dominions of Portugal and under the guns of the castle was entitled to Portuguese protection.

"Van Lloyd's answer was that he was determined to destroy the vessel at the expense of all Fayal and if any protection should be given her by the fort, he would not leave a house standing in the village. All the inhabitants gathered about the walls, expecting a renewal of the attack.

"At midnight, 14 launches were discovered to be coming for the purpose. When they got within clear or gun shot, a tremendous and effectual discharge was made by the privateer which threw the boats into confusion. They now returned a spirited fire but the privateer kept up so continual a discharge that it was almost impossible for the boats to make any progress. They finally succeeded, however, after immense loss, to get alongside of her and attempted to board her at every quarter, cheered on by the officers with a shout of 'No quarter' which we could distinctly hear as well as the shrieks and cries.

"The termination was near-a-bouts a total massacre. Three of the boats were sunk and but one, poor, solitary officer escaped death, in a boat that contained fifty souls. He was wounded. The Americans fought with great firmness, some of the boats were left with but a single man to row them; others with three or four; the most that any returned with was six or eight.

"Several boats floated on shore, full of dead bodies. With great reluctance I state that they were manned with picked men and commanded by the first, second, third and fourth lieutenants of the *Plantagenet;* the first, second, third and fourth ditto of the frigate and the first officers of the brig, together with a great number of midshipmen. Our whole force exceeded 400 men; but three officers escaped, two of which were wounded. This bloody and unfortunate contest lasted about forty minutes.

"After the boats gave out, nothing more was attempted until daylight. The next morning the *Carnation* hauled alongside and engaged her. The privateer still continued to make a most gallant defense. These veterans reminded me of Lawrence's dying words, of the *Chesapeake*—"Don't give up the ship."—The *Carnation* lost one of her top masts and her yards were shot away; she was much cut up in rigging and received several shots in her hull. This obliged her to haul off to repair and to cease firing.

"The Americans, now finding their principal gun (Long Tom) and several others dismounted, deemed it folly to think of saving the privateer against so superior a force. Therefore they cut away her masts to the deck, blew a hole through her bottom, took out their small arms, clothing etc. and went on shore. I discovered only two shot holes in the hull of the privateer, although much cut up in rigging.

"Two boat crews were soon after despatched from our vessels, which went on board, took out some provisions and set her on fire. For three days after, we were employed in burying the dead that washed on shore in the surf. The number of British killed exceeds 120 and

116

90 wounded. The enemy, to the surprise of mankind, lost only 2 killed and 7 wounded. We may well say, 'God deliver us from our enemies,' if this is the way the Americans fight.

"After burning the privateer, Van Lloyd made a demand of the Governor to deliver up the Americans as prisoners. Which the Governor refused. He then threatened to take 500 men on shore and take them by force. The Americans immediately retired, with their arms, to an old Gothic convent, knocked away the adjoining drawbridge, and determined to defend themselves to the last. The Van, however, then thought better than to send his men. He then demanded two men, which he said, deserted from his vessel while in America. The Governor sent for the men but found none of that description.

"Many houses received much injury on shore from the guns of the *Carnation*. A woman, sitting in the fourth story of a house, had her thigh shot off and a boy had his arm broken. The American consul here has made a demand upon the Portuguese government for a hundred thousand dollars for the privateer, which our consul, Mr. Parkin, thinks in justice will be paid; and that they will claim on England.

"Mr. Parkin, Mr. Edward Bayley and other English gentlemen disapprove of this outrage and depredation committed by our vessels on this occasion. The vessel despatched to England with the wounded was not permitted to take a single letter from any person. Being an eye-witness to this transaction, I have given you a correct statement, as it occurred.

"With respect, I am &,
"H.K.F."

AN ABLE SEAMAN OF 1812

(See Adams; also H. A. Fay, "Late Capt. in the Corps of the U.S. Artillerists," *Collection of the Official Accounts, in Detail of all the Battles Fought by Sea and Land, Between the Navy and Army of the United States and the Navy and Army of Great Britain, During the Years 1812, 1813, 1814 & 1815*. New York. Printed by E. Conrad, 1817.)

24. "General Napoleon was a prisoner, on his way to Elba."

It was at the momentary first restoration of the Bourbons. Early in the year the allied nations of Europe invaded France on the eastern frontier, while Wellington pushed up from the south. Napoleon's eagles of victory had flown from his standards and a succession of defeats terminated in his abdication.

The allied statesmen assigned Elba to the dethroned emperor. The next year he escaped, regained his throne for the famous "hundred days," only to lose everything at Waterloo.

25. "If they had known that Gen. And. Jackson was awaiting them, they would have laughed another way."

Although the Treaty of Ghent between Great Britain and the United States was signed in the final weeks of 1814, officially ending the War of 1812, the news of the treaty did not reach New Orleans in time to prevent the decisive defeat of an army of Wellington's veterans, by hastily trained levies under Andrew Jackson. On January 8, 1815, Packingham with 12,000 troops, most of whom had seen service in the Napoleonic wars, and with the watchword "booty and beauty" (Lossing—this is disputed) attempted to capture the city.

It was almost the only land engagement during the second war with England in which the United States forces were victorious. "For, humiliating as it is for the land forces to acknowledge, it is only true and fair to state that hostilities stopped solely on account of political conditions and because of our successful navy" (Ganoe).

26. "They came to anchor direct before the battery at Stonington."

This was a small engagement in a war that was composed of minor battles.

"The whole Atlantic coast was greatly annoyed by small British squadrons during the summer of 1814. These captured many American coasting vessels and sometimes menaced towns with bombardments. In August, Commodore Hardy appeared before Stonington (Conn.) and opened a terrible storm of bombshells and rockets in the town. [The rockets were used to set fire to towns or shipping.] The attack continued four successive days (August 9-12) and several times land forces attempted to debark, but were always driven back by militia.

"The object of this unprovoked attack seems to have been to entice the American force from New London, so that British shipping might go up the Thames and destroy some American frigates near Norwich. This attempt failed and nothing further was ventured on the Connecticut coast" (Lossing).

Durand's Background.

WHEN Durand was born in 1786, the most plentiful article in America was distrust. Each man feared his neighbor; every township was jealous of the next; one state hated all the others. Government, as we now understand it, did not exist.

In the late summer of that year, General Washington invited delegates from all the states to meet at Annapolis to discuss methods of creating a centralized government, which would replace the loose confederation then failing to function. Only five of the states—Virginia, Delaware, New York, New Jersey, and Pennsylvania—sent representatives to the meeting. And those men who met there had about as much actual authority as would the members of the bartenders' union, if they met to-day in St. Louis to discuss the junking or the retaining of the federal constitution.

Jealousies and hatreds which had smouldered through the long years of the Revolution prevented other states from participating at the meeting.

The attitude of the citizens was "Hurrah, we're free!" But with the cheering was no idea of the meaning of freedom. The duty of the government to its citizens and the obligations of the citizens to the government were equally obscure.

121

For instance, in 1784 the army had been reduced to eighty-four men, because "a standing army was subversive to the ideals of a free nation." True, the Indians, maddened by English rum and English gold, were ravaging the frontiers and collecting scalps as a modern schoolgirl collects fraternity pins. The papers were filled with accounts of Indian raids. Nevertheless, Congress resolved "Standing armies are generally converted into destructive engines for establishing despotism: therefore, the commanding officer be, and hereby is directed to discharge the troops . . . except twenty-five privates to guard the stores at Fort Pitt and fifty-five to guard the stores at West Point. . . . No officer to remain in the service above the rank of captain" (Ganoe, *History of the United States Army*).

One wonders why they kept the eighty-four men. They might have discharged them, too, and bought a couple of padlocks for Fort Pitt and West Point.

Two years later, when the army had been increased to about a thousand men, this "legion" was distributed along the frontier from the "Canadas to the Floridas," a fairly thin line of domestic police.

Nothing now existing can equal the remoteness of the frontier cabins and their builders. "News came to them by word of mouth, passed by wandering trappers or during the infrequent gatherings at tavern and church. Their small trading was done by barter. The only money they ever saw was earned by washing black salts from hardwood ashes. They lived

on corn, game, wild roots and fruits or starved. They
did not expose their children to kill off the weaklings,
as did the Spartans. But the cabin chinks let in the
storm and cold of winter until the weaklings died."

Speculators were busy, buying up soldiers' bonus
claims, in anticipation of a raid upon the treasury-
department-to-be. The fortune of at least one United
States senator of to-day dates from his ancestor's
dealings with the impoverished veterans of the Revolution.

It was such wrongs as the pension and pay frauds
that induced Captain Daniel Shays to lead an armed
rebellion before Durand was a year old. Although
sentenced to death, the Captain was never executed
"because he was supported by the great mass of the
people" (Lossing, *History of the United States*).

North hated South as in Civil War times. Western
men hated the East then as an impoverished Nebraska
corn-grower now hates Wall Street. But some way,
some how, affairs went on.

There is no condition of unhappiness, squalor, oppression, or want which the human body can endure
to which the human mind cannot become accustomed.
That fact accounts for the frontiersmen of 1786 and
the infantrymen of 1917.

Strangely enough the states united to better their
conditions, not because of the poverty and misery of
the citizens, but because of the greed of England.
Perhaps the greatest contributing factor in the adop-
tion of the constitution was England's drastic trade

regulation that pinched the commerce between the States and the West Indies. The prominent citizens were hit in the pocketbook and were willing to listen to the forward-looking delegates to the Constitutional Convention. "They realized that, only by concerted action, could they hope to secure Free Trade with the British colonies" (Lossing).

By the time Durand was creeping about the floor of his mother's kitchen, Washington had been elected and inaugurated President of the United States (1789).

How James M'Lean Was Impressed.

A BRIEF story of another seaman's experiences which curiously substantiate and parallel Durand's is to be found in a little, forgotten pamphlet: *"Seventeen Years' History of the Life and Sufferings of James M'Lean,* Written by Himself. Printed for the Author by B & J Russell. Hartford, 1814."

The following paragraphs are clipped from M'Lean's story, which is, for the most part, a dreary account of a seaman's wrongs and sufferings, without a bit of the picturesque color which Durand wove into his story. M'Lean was born in Windsor, Connecticut.

"At the age of ten years I first went to sea and performed several voyages to the West Indies in the merchant service with tolerable success."

He was rescued after a shipwreck near Turk's Island and was brought to New York about the middle of October, 1796, "in a most destitute and naked situation." He made voyages to Liverpool and European ports. Then, upon her return from the mouth of the Congo River in Africa, the brig *Glory-Ann* of Philadelphia put in at the port of Grenada.

"We no sooner let go our anchor than an English man-of-war's boat came on board and pressed me and two more of the seamen and carried us on board the *Madrass*, a fifty-gun ship, commanded by John Dilks, who immediately asked me for my protection.

"I immediately showed him one from a Notary Public in New York by the name of Keyes. The Captain replied, 'I could get one, if I was in America, for half-a-crown, as good as that.' He further said, 'It's no use for you to claim you are an American, for you was born in Scotland.'

"The first lieutenant then stepped up and said, 'Yes, that he was. For I knew his friends in Greenock.' The Captain then made answer, 'He shall then do his duty on the main-top.' . . . The day following I went to the Captain and told him I hoped he would send me on board my own ship as I was an American citizen.

"To which he replied, 'You Scotch rascal, if you do not do your duty, I'll punish you.' . . . Several days after while we were letting a reef out of the main top sail, the sail got tore. The Captain immediately said it was my fault, 'for he is a sulky rascal.'

"He ordered me to be seized and the boatswain's mate to punish me; which he did by giving me twelve lashes on my bare back with the cat-of-nine-tails."

M'Lean was transferred to the *Vengeance* and the ship was sent to Gibraltar to join Lord Nelson's fleet. M'Lean escaped. He shipped on board the *Eliza*, an American ship, and then, about August, 1800, he was on board an American schooner belonging to Boston.

"We fell in with a gale of wind which obliged us to

126

put into Falmouth. While we lay there, I went on shore for water; while watering, an officer came down to the boat with a guard of soldiers. He asked what countryman I was.

"I answered, 'An American.' He told me I must go with him. Upon this he put me into the guard house and ordered the guard to take good care of me. . . . The next morning he sent me on board the *Pique*, frigate. I went to the Captain and showed him my protection. He replied, 'I have plenty like you on board and I do not believe you was ever in any part of the U. States. You are either Scotch or Irish.'

"With that, I pointed out to him the vessel I belonged to and begged him to let me go on board to get my clothes. He said, 'You shan't go, for I'll clothe you.' He ordered a boatswain to see that I did my duty. This was January 17, 1801."

The story here becomes a monotony of floggings, threatened hangings, brutalities, and hardships. Nothing in it is anything more than a repetition of Durand's experiences.

"In January of 1802, one night, while hoisting up our boats, a midshipman came to me and said I did not pull. I told him he could not show me how. He told me, 'You are an insolent rascal' and went off and reported me to the commanding officer. I was immediately put in irons.

"The following day the Captain came on board. . . . all hands were called and I was ordered to strip. They seized me up and gave me twenty-four lashes with a cat-of-nine-tails."

A desertion charge, on account of his former enforced English service, was placed against him. The ship's officers amused themselves by pointing out the fore-yard to him as the place where he would be hung.

"I was put in irons on the lower deck, with nothing to lie on but the bare planks. My allowance was a half-pound of bread, the same quantity of meat and a scanty pittance of water. In this situation I remained until we arrived at St. Helena. On our arrival there I was sent to the main guard house on shore with a pair of irons, weighing fifty pounds on my legs. I continued in this situation fourteen days, during which time I became extremely lowzy and my legs were so swelled, I was unable to move."

He wrote frequently to the American consul in London, and, as in Durand's case, that official could do nothing for the man. M'Lean long afterward, however, learned that once an order was sent to the captain of the ship he was held on, requiring the commander to release him, but the captain must have destroyed the admiralty order.

After more floggings, and after fighting as a British seaman during an expedition against pirates in the Gulf of Persia, M'Lean escaped, helped by the American consul in Portugal.

"After an absence of 17 years, I reached my father's house. You may judge my feelings and their's at the interview. The sympathetic tear could not be suppressed; parental and filial affection were mutually exchanged and every sentiment congenial to friends was endeavored to be reciprocated."

Through British Eyes.

A NEWSPAPER publisher has a standing rule in his editorial room that no athletic victory of a certain university is to be "spread." His objection to news glorifying it dates back many years. Once a coach in charge of that university's football team remarked sagely in his ear, "It's the dirty little tricks that win." The publisher has never forgotten or forgiven that remark.

Perhaps the coach was a descendant of a Yankee navy officer. For the British offer abundant testimony to show that American seamen were full of "dirty little tricks."

It seems to us that the really gross abuses were charged to the English. They were domineering and direct in their methods. They could afford to be, as all the might was on their side. It was not necessary for a British commander to be subtle, if, indeed, any of them were capable of it.

The following paragraphs are taken almost verbatim from the most accessible of English sources, James's *Naval History*. They illustrate the British viewpoint.

Seamen Deserted to Americans.

It is fresh in the recollections of many officers of the British navy, how difficult it was at this period

(1801-1805) to keep the seamen from deserting to the Americans. The short peace of 1803 (British Peace of Amiens with Napoleon) occasioned many of our ships to be paid off; and the nature of the service upon which the Americans were engaged (War with Tripoli) held forth a strong inducement to the manly feelings of the British tar. It was not to raise his arm against his countrymen but against barbarians, whose foul deeds excited indignation in every generous breast.

Americans Decoyed English Sailors.

With respect to seamen, America had, for many years previous to the war, been decoying men from our ships by every artful stratagem. The best of these were rated as petty-officers. Many British seamen had entered on board American merchant vessels. . . .

Except on a few occasions, our battalion marines, although as fine a body of men as any in the two services, had remained comparatively idle. The canker worm neglect had been so long preying upon the vitals of the British navy; but it could not exist among the few ships composing the navy of the United States. America's half-dozen frigates claimed the whole of her attention.

Impressed British Mutinied.

Respecting the fitting out of the *Randolph* it would appear that British sailors were the sufferers on this melancholy occasion.

Mr. Clark says: "The difficulty of procuring American seamen when the frigate was fitting out, obliged Capt. Biddle to comply with a request of a number of British sailors, then prisoners, to allow them to enter on board his vessel. While bearing away from Charlestown, the English sailors, in conjunction with others of the crew, formed the design of taking the ship. When prepared, three cheers were given by them on the gun deck. But by the firm and determined conduct of the captain and his officers, the ringleaders were seized and punished."

The fact that British sailors on board the *Randolph* were trying to regain their liberty proves pretty clearly that, "instead of requesting to enter," the American commander and his officers had, like the authorities on shore, employed coercive means.

Americans Fired on Prisoners through Jail Windows.

This brings to mind a recollection of a circumstance related by an American loyalist, who is now a commissioned officer in His Majesty's land forces. He stated that, when he was confined as prisoner of war in the jail at Philadelphia during the first American war, he frequently witnessed the taking by force of British prisoners of war to man the U. States' vessels then lying in the Delaware.

That, on one occasion, thirty or forty sailors, selected as the most efficient, were dragged forth; and

that, their comrades inside joining in the loud execra-
tions against the authors of such cruelty, the soldiers
appointed to guard the men on their march to the
ships, fired in the jail windows!

Prisoners from Guerrière *Looted.*

The *Constitution's* officers used every art to in-
veigle the *Guerrière's* men into their service. Sixteen
or eighteen, Americans and other foreigners, and
about eight British who had been pressed on their
way to the U. States, remained at Boston (to enter the American navy). . . . When the British called
for their bags, the bags were delivered up nearly
emptied of their contents. . . .

The manner in which the *Java's* men were treated
by the American officers reflected upon the latter in
the highest degree. The moment the poor fellows were
brought on board the *Constitution* they were hand-
cuffed, a thing unknown in our service except upon
urgent necessity and pillaged of everything. [Com-
pare M'Lean's story of being ironed.] True, Lieutenant General Hyslop got back his valuable service
of plate and the other officers were treated civilly.

Who would not rather the governor's plate was
spread out on Commodore Bainbridge's sideboard,
than that the British seamen, fighting bravely for
their country's cause, should be put in fetters and be
robbed of their all?

What is all this mighty generosity but a political

juggle, a tub thrown to the whale? Mr. Madison says to his officers, "Never mind making an ostentatious display of your generosity (except) when you know it will be proclaimed to the world. If you lose anything by it, I'll take care Congress shall recompense you two-fold. Such generous conduct on the part of an American officer of rank will greatly tend to discredit the British statements as to any other acts of yours which are not so proper to be made public. . . ."

One object the *Constitution* officers missed by their cruelty. Only three of the *Java's* men would enter with them; the remainder treated with contempt their reiterated promises of high pay, rich lands and liberty.

Uniformed British Officer Insulted and Attacked.

The last article of the capitulation (of Alexandria) provided that British officers were to see the terms "strictly complied with." One officer sent on this service was a midshipman of the *Euryalus*, a mere stripling.

He strayed some distance from his boat. Two American naval officers rode at him as if to ride him down. One of them, a powerful man, caught His Majesty's midshipman by the shirt collar and dragged him, almost suffocating, across the pummel of his saddle, galloping off with him.

Fortunately the midshipman's shirt collar gave

way and the lad fell to the ground. He quickly ran toward the place where his boat crew was waiting, the American pursuing him. The boat crew was hidden under a bank, so that they could not level their carronade at him. But the minute the American "gentleman" saw the boat's crew, he turned pale with fright and rode off in the contrary direction.

The American editors thought this a good joke and informed us that one of these worthies was Captain David Porter; the other, and he that committed the dastardly assault upon a midshipman in His Majesty's navy was Master-commandant J. Orde Creighton. They were furious at the English because of our entry into Washington a few days before. . . .

Americans Unfair Neutrals.

(From a discussion of causes of the War of 1812)

The hectoring of the Americans exceeded all bounds. Several years experience had taught us that Americans were not over scrupulous in the way of commerce; that is, that, while they were ostensibly FAIR NEUTRALS, the cargo they were carrying would be enemy property, their real destination a prohibited one and all their papers forgeries.

It was thought that a state of OPEN war would improve their morals; that honor, or common honesty at least, would break out among them; that this work of reformation would begin with the Eastern people as they were notoriously of a grave, pious habit. However, two years of war had produced not the slightest effect upon the Boston citizens.

British Seaman Tarred and Feathered in New York.

Shortly after the Declaration of War, Captain Porter ill-used a British subject for refusing to fight against his country. A New York paper, June 27, 1812, gives an account of the transaction.

(The man alleges by affidavit that he was tarred and feathered at Captain Porter's orders, because he refused to take the oath of allegiance to the United States. He says he was cast ashore at the Battery naked, except for the tar and feathers)

Inhuman Methods of Warfare.

Upon her capstan, the *Constitution* mounted a piece resembling seven musket barrels (perhaps the first machine gun). These were fixed together with iron bands. It was discharged with a lock. Each barrel threw 25 balls, within a few seconds of each other, making 145 [?] balls that were shot from the piece within two minutes. The American officers said, "It was intended to act against boarders."

But above all the *Constitution* had on board *a furnace for heating shot.* [Italicized in original.] The American officers said it would heat balls to a white heat in fifteen minutes, but that hot shot "were not to be used in action unless the ship were assailed by a superior force."

What an American officer would call a superior force may be partly imagined!

American Brutality to Prisoners.

Prisoners [from the captured *Levant* and *Cyane*] were kept in the *Constitution's* hold for three weeks, with both hands and legs in irons. They were allowed but three pints of water during the twenty-four hours. When the prisoners were landed at Maranham, five of the *Levant's* boys were missing; upon application and search for them, two were found locked in the cabin of the American Captain of Marines.

[James alleges here that this brutal treatment of prisoners was because they refused to enter the American service.]

The First Dum-dum Bullets.

A desire to torment as well as destroy must have influenced the Americans, or why were the *Chesapeake's* canister shot made up with angular and jagged pieces of iron, broken gun locks, copper nails, etc.?

Many of the *Shannon's* men suffered extremely by being so wounded, especially during the tedious operation of having such abominable stuff extracted from different parts of their bodies.

THROUGH BRITISH EYES

The Americans' Inhuman Chemical Warfare.

A large cask of lime, with the head open, was standing on the *Chesapeake's* forecastle [during the battle in which the *Chesapeake* was captured by the *Shannon* and in which Lawrence lost his life]. It was knocked to pieces by one of the *Shannon's* shot. A bag of this same was found in the fore top. For what precise use this lime was intended has never been fully explained [by the American prisoners]. But the following account of an action before the invention of gun powder may assist the reader in his conjectures.

"The French having invaded England (Henry III, 1217) Hubert de Burgh, Governor of Dover Castle, discovering a fleet of 80 stout ships standing over to the coast of Kent, put to sea with 40 ships. Having gained the wind of them, and having run down some of the smaller ones, he closed with the others. He threw on board a quantity of quick lime, which blowing in their faces, blinded them."

It is true the Americans made no such use of the lime, because a cannon shot scattered the barrel and our brave men, headed by Midshipman Smith came so rapidly and unexpectedly into the fore top before the hellish device could be employed.

*　　　*　　　*

The End